THE AESTHETICS OF SENSUALITY

A STYLISTIC STUDY OF THE POETRY OF KAMALA DAS

N.V. RAVEENDRAN

ATLANTIC

PUBLISHERS & DISTRIBUTORS (P) LTD

Published by

ATLANTIC

PUBLISHERS & DISTRIBUTORS (P) LTD

7/22, Ansari Road, Darya Ganj,
New Delhi-110002
Phones : +91-11-40775252, 23273880, 23275880, 23280451
Fax : +91-11-23285873
Web : www.atlanticbooks.com
E-mail : orders@atlanticbooks.com

Branch Office
5, Nallathambi Street, Wallajah Road,
Chennai-600002
Phones : +91-44-64611085, 32413319
E-mail : chennai@atlanticbooks.com

Printed in India at Nice Printing Press, A-33/3A, Site-IV,
Industrial Area, Sahibabad, Ghaziabad, U.P.

FOREWORD

POETRY, LOVE AND LUST

N.V. Raveendran's study of Kamala Das's poetry is yet another attempt to explicate the works of the author from the theoretical positions recently developed in the West — especially in the light of Western theories of stylistics grounded in modern linguistics. He has, however, used stylistics here as a means of exploring and explaining the poetics of sensuality thereby bridging the gap between language and linguistics on the one hand, and poetry and stylistics on the other. In a way this has helped him to underscore the intensity of the experience the author communicates, in terms of the linguistic resources at her disposal. The author may herself be totally or partially innocent of the technical jargon employed by the critic — but she may in practice corroborate the learned critic's perceptions and insights, which are ultimately derived from the corpus of the texts themselves, and not from abstruse theories. Readers have known for long about the erotic content of these poems, but it was left to Raveendran to demonstrate, with theoretical sophistication and aesthetic involvement, the interconnectedness of aesthetics and stylistics in relation to sensuality. Where the themes are sensual and the presentation sensuous, one cannot resist the temptation to speak about the sensuality of Das's poetics as well.

After two brief and brisk if not hurried, chapters of a general and foundational nature ("Style and the Author" and "Stylistics and Poetry"), Raveendran plunges into his real and delicate task of identifying and establishing the aesthetic consequences of linguistic/stylistic devices employed by Kamala Das. Here he is seen to resort to his own personal responses to the poems as well as non-linguistic theories. There are, therefore, fewer references to linguistics in chapters III and IV. Instead of using purely linguistic insights to get at the meaning of the erotic experience presented in the poems, he seems to follow the more natural and logical course of looking for linguistic explanations for felt literary experiences. He thus bypasses the usual charge against linguistic stylistics that it puts the cart before the horse, and uses language features only to validate and valorize perceptions based on immediate personal responses. Foucault and Heidegger appear to be as helpful as, if not more helpful than, Mukařovský and Leech. Be that as it may, in a majority of poems Raveendran does employ the resources of linguistics and stylistics to explain specific manifestations of the author's innate mastery of the medium. Stylistics is thus made to play its destined and useful role as a mediator between language and literature.

The uniqueness of Kamala Das among Indian English poets, perhaps, is that she is the least academic of them, either in attitude or by training. Nissim Ezekiel was a professor of English, Ramanujan a trained linguist, Parthasarathy a teacher/editor, Jayanta Mahapatra, Shiv. K. Kumar, Arvind Mehrotra etc., are professional academics. Kamala Das being largely self taught, the impression a reader has is that she draws her inspiration from life rather than from library. The power of her poetic utterance comes from its apparent lack of academic sophistication, which is not to say that it lacks a higher kind of subtlety arising from her mother wit. Her homespun English, therefore, may provide a different kind of challenge to the linguist-stylistician. Raveendran has rightly put his finger on a quintessential aspect of Kamala Das's poetic oeuvre in choosing the title for the book "The Aesthetics of Sensuality". In the early decades of this century, Kumaran Asan was considered to have exorcised the ghost of sensual love from poetry, of bodily feelings celebrated in the works of several of his predecessors and could sing of "unstained love". But in our time the body seems to be coming back with renewed vigour — in poetry, drama, fiction and cinema. Few writers are apparently enamoured today of Platonic love. If in much of recent literature love is no more than a metaphor for sensuality it is because its romanticised variety is absent from today's life too. Raveendran here discusses the poetics of sensuality — not of love spiritual or love in the abstract. The language of the body, with any number of four letter word etc., has its own morphology, syntax and lexis as well as devices of parallelism, asyndeton etc. And so has the language of sensual poetry. Call it love or lust — does it really matter, some may ask — Raveendran establishes the validity of his observations on the basis of the language features that reflect and spell out the author's choice of syntagmatic and paradigmatic elements as well as the formal devices and structures of the poems themselves. This attempt is bound to be of value to other scholars as well as students of poetry, of Indian English poetry in particular.

My hearty congratulations to Mr. Raveendran, with best wishes for still greater contribution.

K. AYYAPPA PANICKER

PREFACE

This book attempts to unravel the art and thought of poet Kamala Das, using the tools of stylistics and allied disciplines. The study being 'text-centred' the reader might find his/her knowledge of the formal features of language useful to keep in with the arguments. However, a thorough knowledge of linguistics is not necessary here, as views from other disciplines also have been adopted to make the arguments transparent.

The examination of the stylistic features of the poetry of Kamala Das reveals that while the attempts to construct a personal world goes on there is an apparent parallel attempt at sensual celebration — this celebration underlines her aesthetics of sensuality. This aesthetics of Kamala Das has a universal appeal. In her most personal poems also the poet is found to be sharing with her readers tender emotions. The linguistic manifestations of her impersonal thoughts have shown that the poet's artistry exhibits sameness and diversity. This, it has been found, has to do with her concern for fellow women in particular and humanity in general. All these have been brought to light through detailed stylistic examinations of the texts selected for study. Though I have taken care to justify the method, there might still be some lapses here and there. However, it is expected that the readers will find the analyses within the claims made.

This wouldn't be complete without a mention of the people who at various stages have come forward with support. It was Dr. Joseph's hints that gave me the sense of direction. Surendran's careful reading of the type-script and Madhavan's comments have made my task easier. Prof. K.V. Tirumalesh has generously offered many suggestions. Prof. C.P. Sivadasan of Kannur University has been a benevolent patron. And my salutations to Dr. K. Ayyappa Panicker whose words 'foreground' this book.

N.V. RAVEENDRAN

CONTENTS

1

Style and the Author

Kamala Das's poems that appeared in print from 1965 onwards are both qualitatively and quantitatively impressive and as such they offer enough material for a serious study. Critics and scholars around the world have appreciated the literary merits of her poetry. K.R. Srinivasa Iyengar, the pioneering historian of Indian Writing in English, identifies Kamala Das as "aggressively individualistic of the new poets."[1] H.M. Williams in his survey of Indo-Anglian literature maintains that her poems succeed "because of the identity of feeling and structure."[2] Bruce King observes that Kamala Das "is a natural poet with an excellent feeling for sound, rhythm, phrasing, image, symbol, word play and drama."[3] There are numerous critical surveys of this sort that throw light on the poetic talent of Kamala Das. Her poetry, therefore, deserves a very close stylistic examination.

The relevance of a stylistic study also needs explanation. Roughly speaking, the stylistic study of the work of a writer has two purposes. The first is to inquire into the way thc writer reconstructs his/her experience in the form of a work. The second is to exemplify the effectiveness of the tools used for analysis. Of the two, the former is more important. However, before making any comment on the author's style, the concept of style has to be identified and defined. This is because a stylistic study presupposes a definition of the concepts of style, although the concept itself is elusive. Still, a deliniation of any particular stylistic tool is not indispensable to an attempt like this. This approach is, therefore, based on the assumption that a stylistic study becomes fruitful through a close examination of the artistry of the writer.

Though the works of different writers reflect a style that may exhibit some sort of similarity, scholars are yet to arrive at a unique definition of style. Though there are different concepts of style there is one point about it which has not been disputed : that it is closely related to the use of language in literary creativity. That many theories of style have evolved over the centuries too remains an undisputed fact. It is also true that many doubt the suitability of stylistics as a means of literary interpretation. Stanley E. Fish holds that the practitioners of stylistics, while trying to replace subjectivity "ignore what *is objectively* true — that meaning is not the property of a timeless formalism, but something acquired in the context of an activity — and, therefore, they are more subjective than the critics they would replace."[4] At the same time many believe that stylistics can replace traditional literary criticism. David Lodge says that its purpose is to develop a "more precise, inclusive, and objective methods of describing style than the impressionistic generalizations of traditional criticism."[5] Writers like Helen Vendler think that by using the methods of linguistics the literary analyst can facilitate the comprehension of texts by way of pointing out significant features that traditional criticism fails to note.[6] Again, it is argued that "the operations of ordinary linguistic competence are vital to the meaning and delight of literature."[7] However, mere linguistic competence does not contribute to literary competence. The literary artist's handling of reason, his creative ability, his shaping of experience and his treatment of the motif are not wholly linguistically controlled. The extraordinary dimensions perceivable in a literary work is quite often the outcome of the writer's peculiar sense of choice from everyday experience. When assisted by the analyst's intuition, the understanding of the artist's artistry and the interpretation of art from a scientific angle becomes a fruitful attempt. In spite of this, linguist-critics (like Marvin K.L. Ching) have claimed that a scientific study of the linguistic manipulations of a poet will give new insights into the way the language functions in his/her vision, and also into the way the reader reconstructs this vision.

According to G.N. Leech and M.H. Short style is the way in which language is used in a given context, by a given person, for a given purpose.[8] This is in consonance with Ferdinand de

Saussure's distinction between *langue and parole* — *langue* being the code or system of rulers common to the speakers and *parole* being the particular uses of the system. Style pertains to *parole*, because it is selection from total linguistic repertoire.

The most specific domain of style is the text itself. Leech and Short claim that a text is the nearest one can get to as an example of a homogeneous and specific use of language. They argue that if one thinks of style as "the linguistic characteristic of a particular text" she/he shall be on the safest ground.[9] Further, within a text it is possible to be more specific about how language serves a particular aesthetic function. A 'linguist-critic' may seek to find solutions to problems such as why an author selects a particular way of expression and how a particular aesthetic effect is achieved through language. In this way, literary stylistics is relational in nature. It also relates the critic's concern of aesthetic appreciation with the linguist's concern of linguistic description.

The monist, the dualist and the pluralist approaches are the most predominant among the different approaches to style. The dualist approach rests on an assumed dualism in language, between form and meaning. Dualism is visible in the common definition of style as "way of writing" or a "mode of expression." In the opposite direction there is the monist view of style according to which form is inseparable from content. The opinion of the pluralists differ from both : they view style as functions based on different discourse situations.

Richard Ohmann, who upholds dualism says that "style is a way of writing... In general (it) applies to human action that is partly invariant and partly variable... To put the problem more concretely, the idea of style implies that the words on the page might have been different, or differently arranged, without a corresponding difference in substance."[10] However the model that Ohmann used for his study was an earlier version of transformational grammar (T.G). According to this version optional transformations derive alternate forms of sentences. The theory of T.G. has changed since veering around to the principle that distinction of form implies distinction of meaning.

At the same time, the insight of Ohmann's approach still

holds ground : the basic logical content of a sentence can be represented as a set of elementary propositions, which together with their interrelations constitute its "deep structure" or "semantic representation". The principle of paraphrase (or same meaning in different form) is one which many schools of linguistic thought continue to take for granted as a basic fact of language.[11] However this possibility is limited to everyday use of language. In poetry, every trope confronts with a paraphrase problem, because it denies the reader a literal sense, and so induces him to make sense, that is, to find interpretations beyond the truth-functional meaning captured by paraphrase.[12]

Monism means inseparability of style and content. Stylistic monism finds its strongest ground on poetry where through such devices as metaphor, irony, and ambiguity, meaning becomes complex and sense loses its superficiality.

In pluralism language is viewed as performing a number of different functions and any piece of language is likely to be the result of choices made on different functional levels.[13] Hence the dualist's division between "expression" and "content" is not satisfying to the pluralist. Roman Jakobson is a pluralist who distinguishes six functions (these will be considered later), each corresponding to one essential aspect of the discourse situation. Halliday's functional model of language distinguishes three major functions : "ideational", "interpersonal" and "textual."[14]

Although monism, dualism and pluralism are in conflict with each other and although the term 'style' has suffered from over definition, all these have something to contribute to a comprehensive view of style. In the opinion of Leech and Short, style could be productively used if it is viewed in the following manner :

(1) Style is a way in which language is used : style belongs to *parole* rather than to *langue*. Therefore it consists in choices made from the repertoire of the language.

(2) Stylistics has to do only with literary language.

(3) Viewing style as being relatively *transparent* or *opaque* : transparency implies paraphrasability and

> opacity means that a text cannot be adequately paraphrased and that interpretation of the text depends greatly on the creative imagination of the reader.[15]

'Opacity' is an important feature of poetic language. 'Opacity' comes from deviation from the lexical, grammatical and sematic rules of the language. However, in free-verse, especially those by the Indian writers there is a tension between the opaque and the transparent within the poem. This might have impacts upon the poem's quality.

The foregoing discussion has shown that textual interpretation is the aim of a stylistic approach. However, it must be mentioned that stylistics does not offer a strict methodology to follow. Still, it is clear that a stylistic study can relate textual features to interpretation. In short, modern stylistics can be used to account for the reader's intuitive perceptions of a text in terms of its linguistic features. Thus, in stylistics what produces the result is the interaction between intuition and analysis, and to a considerable extent this is made use of in this study.

NOTES

1. K.R. Srinivasa Iyengar, *Indian Writing in English* (New Delhi : Sterling, 1984) 677.
2. H.M. Williams, *Indo-Anglian Literature 1800-1970* : A Survey (Madras : Orient Longman, 1974) 117.
3. Bruce King, *Modern Indian Poetry in English* (Delhi : Oxford UP, 1987) 147.
4. Stanley E. Fish, "What is stylistics and why are they saying such terrible things about it," *Essays in Modern Stylistics*, ed. Donald C. Freeman (London : Methuen, 1981) 69.
5. David Lodge, *Language of Fiction* (London : Routledge and Kegan Paul, 1967) 52.
6. Helen Vendler, rev. of *Essays on Style and Language* by Roger Fowler, *Essays in Criticism*, 16 (1966) : 457.
7. Marwin K.L. Ching, Michael C. Haley and Ronald F. Lunsford, ed. Introduction, *Linguistic Perspectives on Literature* (London : Routledge and Kegan Paul, 1980) 9.
8. Geoffrey N. Leech and Michael H. Short, *Style in Fiction : A Linguistic Introduction to English Fictional Prose* (London : Longman, 1981) 10.
9. Leech and Short 12.
10. Richard Ohmann, "Generative Grammars and the Concept of Literary Style," *Linguistics and Literary Style*, ed. Donald C. Freeman (New York : Holt Rinehart and Winston, 1970) 258-78.

11. Leech and Short 23.
12. Leech and Short 25.
13. Leech and Short 30
14. M.A.K. Halliday, "Linguistic Function and Literary Style," *Literary Style : A Symposium*, ed. Seymour Chatman (London : Oxford UP, 1971) 330-65.
15. Leech and Short 38-39.

2

Stylistics and Poetry

In Europe, a scientific study of the language of literature began after the publication of *Cours de linguistique gènèrale* (1915) an improved version of Ferdinand de Saussure's unpublished papers on general linguistics. This was a pioneering study on language. The distinction between *la-langue* and *la-parole* — the former the code that makes communication possible among the members of the community, and the latter the way the code is used in actual situation or the individual's competence in expressing ideas linguistically — contain the idea of an impersonal norm, the social function, and the individual's preference.[1]

Charles Bally, a student of Saussure, introduced modern linguistic stylistics in his *Traite de stylistique francise.*[2] According to his model stylistics is the study of expressive effects and mechanism in all language; the only concrete reality being linguistic communication. Excepting the oral transference of moods, everything with in the broad framework of language is, to Bally, mere abstraction. Therefore, according to his theory, literary language is an abstraction, a deviation from the natural language habits. Tabolt J. Taylor summarises the four fundamental principles underlying Bally's approach in the following way :

(1) Like linguistics, stylistics is concerned with how a language makes possible communication of thought.

(2) Thought has two aspects : the conceptual and the non-conceptual. The former is the result of conventions and the latter is the result of personal experience and emotions.

(3) Stylistics should seek to explain how a language adapts to, and makes possible the communications of the subjective, non-conceptual aspects of thought.

(4) Saussure's distinction between langue and parole, syntagmatic and paradigmatic relations delimit expression-forms by taking the perspective of meaningful differences. Different elements of the language would be seen to correlate with different non-conceptual or 'affective' values. This principle will prove to be characteristic of structural stylistic theory as a whole.[3]

In short Bally had tried to exclude literary style from the purview of stylistics and confine it to the study of ordinary speech.

Bally's views on language could initiate a systematic study of the language of literature. However, giving a systematic account of the evolution of stylistics is a difficult task. The developments have occurred in different countries yielding parallel, overlapping or correlated theories. A summary of the important developments in this field is given in the following pages.

New Criticism

Literary conventions in England and America received a shock when, in the beginning of this century, T.S. Eliot, Ezra Pound, James Joyce and W. Lewis focussed their attention on the verbal texture of the literary work and showed an eagerness to dismiss conventional literary judgement as obsolete. This approach soon gained popularity and became a method of style study in its broadest sense. Within a short period it found its way to Cambridge where scholars like I.A. Richards and William Empson developed it further through studies on Practical Criticism, and Ambiguity. Richards demonstrated how the literary text can be interpreted through a close study of verbal texture. William Empson's interest was in exemplifying plurality of meaning which he did in his book *Seven Types of Ambiguity*.[4] The textual criticism of the Cambridge Circle was shipped to America where it formed the basis of New Criticism, or stylistic criticism.

The New Criticism shared with the French *explication de*

texte a liking for a close reading of the text investigating relation between aesthetic responses and the stimuli in the text. The strength in the attempts of the New Critics was that their investigation of poetic structure and technique was thorough and their weakness was in their neglect of a detailed cultural and linguistic examination. The New Criticism, though it was "lively and envigourating" soon tended to be "an extremely undisciplined affair, strangely innocent of scholarship."[5]

German Stylistics

The Germanic writers had attempted to study the language of individual works right from the beginning of this century. Their attempts begin with Benedetto Croce and Karl Vossler. While Croce investigated linguistics as a part of aesthetics[6] Vossler sought linguistic clues to national cultures.[7] As opposed to the work of Bally's school, the German stylistics — Stilforschung — takes the intuition of the writer into consideration and avoids linguistic classification. Leo Spitzer, a major practitioner of the Germanic school, emphasizes the supreme function of language in the text by giving it a metaphorical definition, "the life blood of the poetic creation."[8]

Though linguists accuse Spitzer of having no method to offer for investigation of literature, his approach is an example of stimulus based stylistic study of text. Spitzer says that a thorough examination of the language of the text will enable the reader to know the "inward life-centre of the work of art."[9] The literary analyst must begin with an observation of the superficial appearance of the work, and "then grouping these details and seeking to integrate them into a creative principle which may have been present in the soul of the artist; and finally making the return trip to all the other groups of observations in order to find whether the 'inward form' one has tentatively constructed gives an account of the whole."[10]

The essential of Spitzer's method is what he calls the "philogical circle." An important feature of this method is that the initial observation is needed to be spontaneous intuitive insight : some authentic connection between the observer and the work of art must establish itself spontaneously. Hence it must be noted that according to spitzer's theory one who is not intuitively attached to literature cannot be a literary analyst.

The approaches of French and Germanic schools do not dwell upon any single stylistic aspect or try to suggest any particular tool of universal applicability. What follows, therefore, is a consideration of the ideas of those that suggest specific tools for stylistic analysis.

Russian Formalism

The contribution of the *Russian Formalists* to the theory of literature was great. The theory of *defamiliarization (ostranenie)* was propounded by Viktor Sklovskij. Technique of art, in his view, "is to make objects 'unfamiliar', to make forms difficult, to increase the difficulty and length of perception because the process of perception is an aesthetic end itself and must be prolonged."[11] The reader who is attached to clichés, stock responses and automatised perceptions is given a formally defamiliarized pattern. This defamiliarized pattern (poetic) portrays things as if they are seen for the first time and hence brings about a heightened awareness of the world. The origin of this theory could be traced back to Aristotle who in *Poetics* says : "the unfamiliarity due to this deviation from normal usage will raise the diction above common place, while the retention of some part of the normal forms will make for clarity."[12]

The formalists studied literature from a formal view point : they concentrated on the text and looked at poetic language as a 'deviant' form of the standard. It was Sklovskij who developed this from his own notion of estrangement. Formalists like Ejxeubaum, Tynjanov, Tomasvskij and Jakubinskij accepted this.

'Defamiliarization' (ostranenie) is synonymous with 'de-automatization' and 'marking strange'. The confusion arising out of the use of the terms 'defamiliarization' and 'making strange' has two dimensions. First, it would mean the description of the literary devices found in the actual text. Second, it would point out the effect of those devices upon the reader. These two meanings are not distinguished — the proponents of formalism have blended them. It would be worth mentioning here that certain estrangement from the norms of the so called "public language'' is a fundamental characteristic of art, because art cannot depict life as it is. But this device could be productively employed to capture aspects of the 'remoteness' of poetic language.

Structuralism

Structuralism which is defined as ''a mode of analysis of cultural artifacts which originates in the methods of contemporary linguistics''[13] has its roots in Ferdinand de Saussure. The Prague linguistic circle contributed greatly to structural linguistics and stylistics. The term 'foregrounding' which denotes a very effective stylistic tool is a translation of Czech 'aktualisace'.[14] The linguist critic Havránek brought forth a functional differentiation of the standard language on the basis of three processes : intellectualization, automatization and foregrounding. On the basis of these three processes he differentiated language into three modes : *Scientific language* where functional accuracy is aimed at, *everyday language* which is meant for everyday communication; *poetic language* which is characterized by the foregrounding devices.[15] The identification of poetic language as 'foregrounded' does not suggest that poetic language is wholly foregrounded, because it cannot exist without the automatized (core) language. A summary of the views of the chief proponents of structuralism will give insight into the structuralist contribution to stylistics.

One of the chief proponents of structural stylistics is Jan Mukařovský. In his ''Standard Language and Poetic Language''[16] Mukařovský points out that the essence of poetic language lies in the violations of the norms of the standard language. The Prague scholar says that the systematic violation of the standard language is what makes possible the poetic utilization of language.

Mukařovský conceives that foregrounding results due to the deviation of a given component from current use. If all components deviate there is no foregrounding because ''a complete foregrounding of all the components is impossible.''[17] This view has been questioned by practitioners of literary stylistics like Anne Cluysenaar.[18] Cluysenaar's argument is that in poetry, the background being the norms of the standard language and since the standard language is outside the poetic work, different elements of the work could be simultaneously foregrounded.[19] Still we cannot overlook the concept because of the insight it shows into the study of poetic language.

It was shown that the aesthetic structure of the poem arises out of foregrounded features. It was also shown that the literary variety of the standard language is the common core. In poetic language, since total foregrounding is impossible, certain elements lie in the back-ground and any change in this state will affect the structure of the work. Foregrounding effected this way is visualized as deviation from the everyday usage — deviation either of the standard language or of the poetic conventions of a given time.

Muařovský, following Jungmann, points out "uncommonness" or distortedness as a characteristic feature of poetic language.[20] He notices unexpectedness, unusualness and uniqueness[21] as the basic feature of poetic neologisms. In other words these are special characteristics of foregrounding. Though ordinary speech also contains a high amount of foregrounding such as onomatopoeia, similes and metaphors, use of foreign words etc., in all such cases, says Mukařovský, foregrounding devices are used to attract the attention of the reader to the communication situation.

The point where a serious doubt arises in Mukařovský's discussion of foregrounding is the distinction between attention calling to subject-matter and to the speech event. Similarly the distinction between the 'structured' and 'unstructured' aesthetic is difficult to comprehend.

If Mukařovský's concern was the way poetic language deviated from the norms of the standard language, it was on *parallelism* that Roman Jakobson concentrated his attention. Beginning with the elementary factors that constitute a speech event Jakobson argues that a 'code' must establish a 'contact' between the 'addresser' and the 'addressee'. This 'addresser' 'addressee' relationship should be such that a 'message' should refer to a 'context' in reality. The nature of the communicative situation is determined by the degree of emphasis laid on one or other of these six factors. Based on this emphasis Jakobson distinguishes six different functions of language. Thus, if the emphasis is on the addresser the function is *emotive*; if it is on the context the function is *referential;* if the purpose of speech is social contact the function is *phatic*; when the code itself is prominent the function is *metalingual;* when the addressee is important the function is *conative* and if the message itself is the main point of concern the function is *poetic*.[22]

Jakobson points out that the 'set' towards the message is crucial for the poetic function to become active.[23] This according to W.V. Peer, means "that the reader, as a participant in the act of literary communication, is 'set' towards poetic function." Further, "in reading poems people tend to be geared towards the parallelisms, and to find aesthetic reward in them, while they might not adopt such a set when reading prose."[24]

Jakobson argues that poetic function is the proper subject matter of literary studies. While in ordinary speech situation different kinds of elements are found in the syntagmatic chain, poetic language exhibits repeated combinations of 'same' kinds of elements. This repetition of equivalents is called parallelism. In Jakobson's theory with parallelisms of sound, stress, image, and rhyme a poet foregrounds the formal qualities of his poem while sequential, discursive and referential meaning lie in the background.

While Jakobson considers stylistics as the study of verbal art, Michael Riffaterre, a member of Jakobson's school, views stylistics in a different way — his views are reader based. Literary style, according to Riffaterre, arises out of the author's encounter with how to surmount the difficulties that are encountered in the communication of his message to the reader.

In his study of poetic language[25] Riffaterre says that the semantic indirectness of a poem is produced by displacing, distorting, or creating meaning. When one word stands for the other there is 'displacing' as in the case with a metaphor or metonymy. When there is ambiguity, contradiction or non-sense it is a case of 'semantic distortion'. When meaning is created by symmetry or rhyme it is a case of 'meaning creation.'[26]

If reality could be represented only through the referentiality (direct relationship of word to meaning) then the deviant language of poetry does not represent reality. This follows that it is through misrepresenting reality (in a way defamiliarizing) that poets make meaning. Thus, the poet "multiplies details and continually shifts its focus to achieve acceptable likeness to reality."[27] Mimesis in poetry is then variation and multiplicity. This argument takes us to the reader's competence and how the poetic text is interpreted.

The first stage of reading (a poem) leading to interpretation is syntagmatic unfolding, that is, reading from top to bottom of the page. It is in this reading that meaning is apprehended. The reader's linguistic competence (which is referential) contains his ability to perceive incompatibilities between words :

...to recognise that a word or a phrase does not make literal sense, that is it makes sense only, if he (and he is the only one around to do it) performs a semantic transfer, only if he reads that word or phrase as a metaphor, for example, or as a metonymy.[28]

The text is *linear* and the deciphering process or interpretation is *bilinear*. The reader's knowledge of the language or his linguistic competence enables him to perceive the ungrammaticality of a poetic text. The ungrammaticalities stem from the fact that a phrase has been generated by a word that should have excluded it. It could also stem from the fact that the poetic verbal sequence is characterized by contradictions between the word's presuppositions and its entailments.

Linguistic competence, however, is not the only factor that enables interpretation. Literary competence is also determined by the reader's familiarity with descriptive systems, with themes, his knowledge about myths and his familiarity with other texts. Hence, according to Riffaterre, a pure linguistic study is not enough for a satisfactory interpretation of any poetic work. To the sort of reading described above Riffaterre gives the name *heuristic reading.*

At the second stage of interpretation what the reader does is the *hermeneutic* reading. In this stage of reading the reader remembers what he has just read and modifies his first reading in the light of what he is now decoding, that is, as he re-reads the text he comes to recognize that successive and differing statements which he noted as ungrammaticalities in his first reading, are variants of the same structural matrix. In this the interpreter reveals that :

The text is in effect a variation or modulation of one structure

— thematic, symbolic, or whatever — and this sustained relation to one structure constitute the (poem's) significance.[29]

The poetic writers, though the text's mimetic accuracy is verifiable, distorts facts or at least shows a bias in favour of details which may converge possibly metonymically on a single concept. The interpretational stages that Riffaterre suggests, are, therefore, intended to reveal the meaning distorted in this way.

Equating stylistics with expressive features Stephen Ullmann draws similarity between stylistics and linguistics. His studies strengthen the argument that both the "expressive and the cognitive" are stylistic. Ullmann takes a particular device in a literary language and examines the various effects which result from it.[30] Taken as devices leading to the explanation of various effects, imagery, metaphor, simile, metonymy etc. can serve as a focal point around which various effects are produced. These devices transcribe highly complex abstract experiences in concrete terms; they serve as vehicle of irony, imply other value judgements, play their part in the linguistic portrayal of character and have all kinds of other functions.

Ullmann's approach to stylistics is based on form meaning dichotomy. His treatment of stylistics as an independent discipline and the identification of the three level structure like the three components — phonology, syntax and semantics — in T.G. are a furtherance of his own dualistic approach based on semantics.

Placing semantics in one of the three levels of stylistics Ullmann identifies the 'expressive' values which some semantic features may acquire.[31] Ullmann locates these expressive values in the semantic relation between words. Of these the simple semantic situations — 'motivation' of theme, vagueness of sense and the overtones — have significant stylistic corollaries.

Though he distinguishes 'motivation' into phonetic, morphological and semantic, it is semantic motivation that is given importance. This is because semantic motivation is the more frequent kind in literature. Metaphor, metonymy and similar devices are motivated by the connection that exists between literal and the transferred meaning. The metaphor is of fundamental importance in style for two reasons. Firstly, by combining a tenor and a vehicle metaphor (and simile) produce a kind of double vision — two ideas for one. Secondly, an image of some worth discovers a hidden analogy between a seemingly disparate phenomena — jaxtaposing the disparate. Thirdly, metaphor offers freedom of choice which is otherwise restricted (there is a limit to freedom in the grammatical and lexical choices). The only sphere where the author can choose with unlimited freedom is imagery, because any tenor (the subject we are talking about) may be compared to any vehicle (the element to which the tenor is compared).

Vegueness of meaning has often been denounced by poets as a major short coming in language. However, in many situations the presence of vagueness and precision is of aesthetic value, because vague expressions give free scope to imagination and precision offers a counterpoint.

Replacing the disputed term, 'emotive' with 'connotations' or 'overtones' Ullmann speaks about three groups of this category : overtones connected with the name, sense and particular register. The presence of a foreign word, a proper name or a neologism may give rise to pleasant or unpleasant overtones. Hence, the aesthetic effect of the names of mythological figures like Radha, or Krishna may reinforce their association with the theme of the poem. "Gawky," "grumpy," "squawk" etc., are words whose actual meaning contains an element of evaluation — these give sense to overtones connected with sense. Overtones associated with particular register or the 'evocative value' encounters the basic dichotomy between 'colloquial' and 'formal' language. Thus evocative overtones can arise from differences in space (regional, dialectal, foreign elements), or in time (archaisms, neologism), those between the speeches of different sexes and the like. According to Ullmann, such identifications and explanations give the meaning of a literary text.

The British Approach

The British linguists have endeavoured to study the applicability of linguistics in literary interpretation. They have developed a few descriptive strategies, and identified certain interpretational constraints. The main contributions of this school are the devices of cohesion, prominence and internal and external deviation. There are also attempts to view the theory of foregrounding as a pragmatic concept.

G.N. Leech, the British linguist-critic seeks to differentiate sharply between linguistic description and critical interpretation. In one of his papers Leech analyses Dylan Thomas's poem "This Bread I Break" bringing out the lexical and grammatical means which the poet draws from standard language to unify the poem.[32] He relates this cohesion to the foregrounded elements in the poem. This cohesion of foregrounding is a powerful interpretational constraint.

Leech observes that foregrounding may occur due to deviational (paradigmatic — introduction of a paradigm) or parallelistic (syntagmatic — repetition of the same element) nature of the poem. These two mutually opposing processes could be united through the principle of selection. Leech says that for a poetic piece to carry aesthetic value, there must exist a cohesion between deviational and parallelistic elements.

M.A.K. Halliday's "systemic grammar" describes the nominal groups, the lexical sets and cohesive devices in the literary text.[33] His aim is to demonstrate the way the language of literary texts can be described according to linguistic categorization and not to relate those linguistic factors to aesthete effects. Halliday defines his concept of prominence as deviation or parallelism. If a poetic line shows a concentration of a certain phonemes, their recurrence constitutes prominence. To be understood as real foregrounding the prominent items have to be motivated either by the subject matter or by the meaning of the text as a whole. Hence, the presence of deviance or parallelism is not in itself a sure means to interpretation.

Taking the cue from the T.G. framework S.R. Levin distinguishes between 'external' and 'internal' deviation.[34] External deviation is violation of the norm outside the poem such as grammar, norms of writing poetry, violation of traditional subject matter, and violation of the cultural and aesthetic norms of a society. Internal deviation occurs against the background of the poetic text itself. Levin distinguishes external deviation into 'determinate' and 'statistical' deviation.[35] Determinate deviation results from the breaking of a linguistic rule or the violation of a cultural code. Statistical deviation arises when in poetry there occurs a deviation due to the high degree of unexpectedness, that is, the use of a linguistic element in a *context* where the probability of its occurrence is low. Thus, the deviant element draws the attention of the reader to some particular aspect. However, the effectiveness of this element depends upon the context because in a different context its effect would be nothing.

Viewing foregrounding as a pragmatic concept, W.V. Peer attempts to evolve an integrated theory of foregrounding. Explaining his view Peer refers to the dynamic interaction involving the author, the literary text and the reader.[36] To the reader foregrounding devices are a guiding factor as well as a source of aesthetic satisfaction. The experience that the reader is subjected to while reading the poem and his perception of the textual elements form the foreground and background that crate the tension. Within this field of tension the reader continually constructs relationship between the foreground and background.

The text is the medium of interaction between the author and the reader. Since this interaction is indirect, the reader's understanding of the text will be influenced by all kinds of negative factors, thereby making his interpretation impressionistic to a considerable extent. However, the devices of foregrounding restrict the readers' interpretation from running wild. Two such foregrounding devices that can limit the number of interpretations are deviation and parallelism. Deviation (the three kinds, discussed already) and parallelism may occur on each of the three linguistic levels — phonology, syntax and semantics. Thus foregrounding becomes multidimensional, the four devices operating on each of the three levels.

The impact of these devices will be influenced by their 'density' and their 'cohesion'. In the linear organization of the text a series of similarities created by a series of devices which limit the interpretative possibilities may be present. This pertains to the cohesive aspects of the text. Simultaneous occurrence of foregrounding devices at phonological, syntactic and semantic levels may create a nexus of foregrounding at one or other points in the text. At such points of density, in cooperation with cohesion, takes shape the focal point which exercises profound influence upon the interpretative and evaluate operations of the reader.

Before we pass on to the generative/pragmatic approach a word about the Indian approach to literary style seems to be necessary. The attitude of the ancient Sanskrit scholars towards literary style is qualitatively different from that of their European counterparts. Though stylistics is nowhere found as a separate field of study in Indian literary tradition, a tendency is seen to describe poetic language in terms of linguistic elements with which it is constituted. This is apparent in the works of Ananda Vardhana and Kuntaka.

In Sanskrit poetics there exists a theory which can be legitimately called theoretical stylistics. Unlike the impressionistic literary analysts of the ancient west the Sanskrit commentators focused on relating the sort of delight one gets from reading a piece of literature to the layout of the linguistic elements in the poem. In their attempt to point out those peculiarities of verbal display they describe the literary, the aesthetic and the emotive devices available to the poet. Ananda Vardhana's treatise on 'dhvani' or suggestive language distinguishes style features at the level of phonemes (varna), morphemes (padaikadesa), and word combinations (pada-racana).[37] In short, characterization classification and naming of parts constitute the main features of the Ananda Vardhana school of poetics.

The description of stylistic tools assumes a different magnitude in Kuntaka. In his treatise on Vakrokti he discusses stylistic features ranging from the arrangement of syllables to the study of the text as a whole. Kuntaka takes into consideration lexical, syntactic and semantic deviation to determine the worth of a literary work. For him "poetry is that word and sense together enshrined in a style revealing the 'out of the way' creativity of the poet on the one hand and giving aesthetic delight to the man of taste on the other."[38] It is that quality of the poem which induces delight in the reader (which is the end of poetry according to the classical Indian approach). It is the product of subtle imagination, which when manifest in words would appeal to the aesthetic faculty of the "man of taste". Kuntaka shows that through the use of deviant syntax and figures of speech like tropes, even trivial subject-matter can be elevated to subtlety. Thus, Kuntaka's discussion of the language of poetry shows some useful means of analysis and appreciation.

The Generative Approach

Generative grammar purports to represent the logical principles of the relation between propositional language structures and predictable semantic effects. However, a total reliance on this school of linguistics has been ruled out by many. Marvin K.L. Ching and associates propose the use of the following components for a linguistic theory of interpretation :

(1) The generative transformational core, stipulating the logical truth conditions and principles of meaning amalgamation from formal propositions; this component, without reference to the actual psychological process of perception and meaning selection, would elaborate all possible semantic effects which constitute the range of meaningful choices the reader constructs either consciously or unconsciously from discrete, explicit, sentential units.

(2) The pragmatic overlay, stipulating the formal rules of textual and contextual induction and deduction from implicit linguistic relationships; these components, again without any necessary empirical basis in psychology, would elaborate the range of possible hidden meanings or other meanings arising from relationship larger than discrete, explicit sentences.[39]

The use of the generative and pragmatic approaches in studying poems written in this century is particularly relevant. Though poets like Shelley had contended that a poem is a non-translable and non-paraphrasable piece, the very fact that it is written to be read presupposes the need for comprehension and interpretation. The attitude of the twentieth century poets further elaborates the scope of a stylistic interpretation. The poems of this century are created out of something more basic than the poems of the past. The truth in this approach is made obvious by the modern poet's tendency to tell that the sounds, the words, the sentences and the language — text structures — are not only a way of telling about things, but also a way of seeing things.

The early 'transformational stylisticians' like Richard Ohmann were interested in giving formal, empirical and quantitative data in support of established critical opinion.[40] But the attempts of Ohmann and others were to develop methods rather than results. William O. Hendricks[41] suggested a hybrid discipline which is neither linguistics nor-literary criticism. He calls it *stylolinguistics*, a term used by Nils Eric Enkvist[42] too. This discipline can offer a co-ordinated study of interrelationship of the areas common to both.

The transformationalists posit two levels of meaning :

(1) Propositional meaning — that meaning which can be represented in an underlying structure.

(2) Pragmatic meaning — the context induced meaning which is added to the propositional meaning.

Thus, they argue that transformations do not change meaning.

The generative semanticists believe in Pascal's dictum that "words differently arranged have different meaning."[43] Hence, to the generative semanticists two different surface structures have different meanings. So, stylistic variations in the surface structure cannot be accounted for without some additional component to separate transformations which effect content changes from those which effect stylistic changes. However, the speech-act theory with its distinction between what a sentence says (locution) and what it may be used to do (illocution) may give insight into the semantic and aesthetic effects of literary style. Since these are different theoretical and methodological models the approach of the literary analyst becomes eclectic.

Thus, the literary analyst who wishes to use linguistics for his study will be tempted to consider the various theories and methods as choices available to him. No model can be dismissed as useless unless it fails to evolve the predicted results and even a correct model is inadequate if its objectives are incomplete. A model, however, may claim to formalise all aspects of human communication. This, however, is not a point for us to ponder as no model is complete in its present state.

The literary analyst may make use of the tools of either the structural or the transformational linguist. The data analysed by the structural linguist are empirical rather then intuitive. Structuralism is essentially a performance model, a way of formalising the patterns of those utterances which already happen to exist. But in contrast generative grammar is a competence model, a way of formalising not just the patterns of given utterances, but the principles governing our understanding of the potentially utterable. This model offers a unique perspective, a way of seeing how the aesthetic creativity of the literary artist depends in part upon and interacts with the rational creativity of an ordinary reader.

The Pragmatic Approach : Speech Acts

The basic insight in 'speech Acts' or 'illocutionary' acts originally proposed by J.L. Austin[44] and developed by J.R. Searle[45] is that language use has an extra dimension which has been some what neglected by logicians and linguists — a performative dimension. The linguist is interested in how language encodes meanings, and in such semantic properties as well-formedness, ambiguity, contradiction, tautology etc., the logician in the conditions for the truth or falsehood of the propositions expressed in languages and in logical relationships between propositions and truth criteria.

Searle considers speech-act theory as a rule governed activity.[46] Utterances fall into three general categories : the proposition bearing statements called constative utterances, the "performative" utterances which are not subject to the notions of truthfulness or falsehood, and "executive" use of language, that is, the use of verb phrases comprising the first person singular pronoun, and simple present indicative verbs. In a delivery of a single utterance three types of act namely locutionary act, illocutionary act and perlocutionary act may be performed. Locutionary act is the basic act of producing a meaningful utterance in the speaker's language in accordance with the syntactic, phonological, and morphological, and all the other relevant factors of speech. Illocutionary act is the very purpose of making an utterance; saying something, asking questions, ordering someone to do something, promising, asserting the truth of a proposition etc. Here the speaker's intention to reveal his thought to others is meant. It is the illocution that constitutes the speech-act proper. Perlocutionary act is performed by means of saying something, convincing one's interlocutor, moving him to anger, and so on. The effect created on the interlocutor is called the perlocutionary effect.[47]

Participants in speech events are engaged in a form of interaction, which means that they not only share a common language and more or less similar logical and epistemological principles but also have an agreed end in view, that is, the achievement of an effective and coherent exchange. H.P. Grice observes that the successful conduct of linguistic interaction is possible only on the basis of a joint commitment to the communicative objective.[48] Grice formulates this as a global conversational rule, which he names the conversational principle.[49] He argues that the exchange is regulated by indispensable principles of decorum allowing coherence and continuity. These principles are stated as maxims implicitly governing the participant's contributions.[50]

1. *The maxim of quantity.*

(a) The contribution should be informative as is required for the purpose of exchange. (b) The contribution should not be more informative than required.

2. *The maxim of quality.*

This maxim is expressible as the super maxim 'Try to make the contribution one that is true'. (a) The speaker should not say what he knows to be false. (b) He should not say that for which he lacks evidence.

3. *The maxim of relation.*

This asks the speaker to 'Be relevant'.

4. *The maxim of manner.*

This is expressible as super maxim 'Be perspicuous'. (a) The speaker should avoid obscurity. (b) He should avoid ambiguity. (c) He should avoid unnecessary prolixity. (d) He should be orderly.

Grice goes on to show how the speaker may exploit the maxims in order to mean more than what he says — it is on these conversational rules that 'unspoken' meanings are often understood.

"Implicatures" may come out of the conscious or unconscious breaking or the exploiting of the maxims. If the listener is an active participant he will easily understand the implicature.

Grice holds that irony, metaphor, meiosis and hyperbole can be analysed in terms of conversational implicatures. They all result from the violation of the maxim of quality : "Do not say what you believe to be false." The salient feature of a figurative utterance, as Grice views it, is that it is false. The hearer (the reader) concludes that the speaker (the poetic persona) must have been attempting to get across some closely related proposition which does not violate the maxim of truthfulness : in the case of irony, for example, it might be the contrary of what is said, and in the case of metaphor it might be a comparison, so that metaphor is re-interpreted as implicating a simile. The stylistic application of speech act thereof and Gricean maxims is that they help in characterising an author's style in terms of speech acts, and thereby participate in the task of interpretation.

To sum up, literature is man's never ending attempt to shape his life through language. Hence, there is no final attempt in its interpretation. Many practitioners believe that linguistic study of literature has revealed the very nature of language of literature. It has nevertheless helped the study of interrelationship of some of the syntactic, semantic and figurative resources. It has helped readers' comprehension of the literary work through explaining the tension between form and content and the deliberate distortion of syntactic and semantic aspects. It has also helped describing the nature of ambiguity and the various meanings the reader may ascribe to a word, phrase or a sentence. It is in this vein that we consider this approach to literary interpretation relevant. As already noted, this study does not rely wholly on the methods of linguistics. Intuitive perceptions, and theories related to the themes will have no less serious place in the succeeding chapters : the study does not follow a definite model, but aims at a definite purpose, that is, the creation of a new model.

NOTES

1. See Ferdinand de Saussure, *Cours de linguistique gènèrale*, ed. Charles Bally and Albert Sechehaye (Paris : Payot, 1955).

2. Bally's theory is discussed in Tobolt J. Taylor, *Linguistic Theory and Structural Stylistics* (Oxford : Pergamon Press, 1980).
3. Taylor 20-21.
4. See William Empson, *Seven Types of Ambiguity* (London : Chatto and Windus, 1930).
5. Graham Hough, *Style and Stylistics* (London : Routledge and Kegan Paul, 1969) 18.
6. See Benedetto Croce, *Estetica como scienza dell' espressione linguistica generale* (Palermo : Sandron, 1904).
7. See Karl Vossler, *Frankreichs Kultur in Spiegel seiner Sprachentwicklung* (Heidelberg : Carl Winter, 1913).
8. Leo Spitzer, *Linguistics and Literary History : Essays in Stylistics* (Princeton : Princeton UP, 1948) 18.
9. Spitzer 19.
10. Spitzer 19.
11. L.T. Lemon and M. Reis, *Russian Formalist Criticism : Four Essays* (Lincoln : Nebraska UP, 1965) 12.
12. T.S. Dorsch, *Classical Literary Criticism* (Harmondsworth : Penguin, 1965) 63.
13. Jonathan Culler, *Structuralist Poetics : Structuralism, Linguistics and the study of Literature* (London : Routledge and Kegan Paul, 1975) 4.
14. See P. Gravin, *A Prague School Reader on Esthetics, Literary Structure and Style* (Washington : Georgetown UP, 1964).
15. See Gravin.
16. See Jan Mukařovský, "Standard Language and Poetic Language," *Essays on the Language of Literature, eds.* Seymour Chatman and S.R. Levin (New York : Houghton Mifflin Company, 1967) 241-49.
17. Mukařovský, "Standard Language" 243.
18. See Anne Cluysenaar, *Introduction to Literary Stylistics* (London : Batsford, 1976).
19. Cluysenaar 61.
20. Mukařovský, "Standard Language" 247.
21. Mukařovský, 248.
22. Roman Jakobson, "Closing Statement : Linguistics and Poetics," *Style in Language, ed.* T.A.. Sebeok (Cambridge, Mass : M.I.T. Press, 1960) 350-77. See especially page 357.
23. Jakobson 356.
24. W.V. Peer, *Linguistics and Psychology : Investigations of Forgrounding* (London : Croom Helm, 1986) 13.
25. See Michael Riffaterre, *Semiotics of poetry* (1978; London : Methuen, 1980).
26. Riffaterre 2.
27. Riffaterre 2.
28. Riffaterre 5.
29. Riffaterre 6.
30. Stephen Ullmann, *Meaning and Style* (Oxford : Basil Blackwell, 1973) 83.

31. Ullmann 40-63.
32. Geoffrey N. Leech, "This Bread I Break" — Language and Interpretation," Freeman 119-128.
33. M.A.K. Halliday, "Descriptive Linguistics in Literary Studies," Free man 57-72.
34. S.R. Levin, "Internal and External Deviation in Poetry," *Word*, 21 (1965) : 226
35. S.R. Levin, "Deviation — Statistical and Determinate in Poetic Language, " *Lingua.* 12 (1963) : 276-90.
36. Peer 20-23.
37. Ashok Aklujkar, "Stylistics in Sanskrit Tradition," *Current Trends in stylistics,* eds. Braj B. Kachru and Herbert F.W. Stahlke (Edmonton : Linguistic Research Inc., 1972) 5.
38. K. Krishnamoorthy, trans., *Vakrokti Jeevita of Kuntaka* (Dharwad : Karnataka University, 1977) 292.
39. Ching, Haley, and Lunsford 16-17.
40. See Fish 53-78.
41. For a consideration see Ching, Haley and Lunsford 22.
42. See Nils Erick Enkvist, *Linguistic Stylistics* (The Hague, Paris : Mouton, 1973).
43. W.F. Trotter, trans. *Pensee,* by Pascal (New York : Modern Library, 1941) 11.
44. J.L. Austin, *How to Do Things with Words* (New York : Oxford UP, 1962).
45. J.R. Searle, *Speech Acts : An Essay in the Philosophy of Language* (Cambridge : Oxford UP, 1969).
46. Searle 12.
47. See Searle 22-53.
48. H.P. Grice, "Logic and Conversation," *Syntax and Semantics Vol. 3, Speech Acts*, eds. Cole and Morgan (New York : Academic Press, 1975) 45.
49. Grice 45.
50. See Grice 41-58.

3

The Aesthetics of Sensuality

This chapter discusses how Kamala Das expresses her poetic self imbued with sensuality through various stylistic devices. The analysis begins with the assumption that a poet is an originator of an utterance with a predominantly aesthetic orientation and that a poem is the product of the sum total of the poet's experiences artistically rendered.[1] The work always presents certain image of the personality of the writer both through direct statements and through its entire structure.[2] However, a writer cannot write without having read works by other people and thus will be influenced in one way or other.

The individual responses to the history of the times and the fresh developments in the area of women's literature play a vital role in shaping the sensibility of a woman writer. Woman's sexual freedom has been the main topic of women writers for about two hundred years. The tendency has been to demand freedom for self expression in all fields. In literature the main theme has been women's right for seeking sexual pleasure of choice, through heterosexuality or lesbianism. In Kamala Das's case, while the same trend underlines her aesthetics, there is the influence of the Indian erotic literature also. The projection of the writer's individuality, while being a common trend among the modern women writers, has a special flavour in her case. A writer like Kamala Das always feels an urgency to project and assert her individuality : much of her poems will, then, show the presence of such syntactic and semantic devices as may convey to the reader her thoughts and emotions. The poems analysed in this chapter will show how the poet's individuality and her aesthetics are presented through various formal devices. However, the fact that a poetic piece is not necessarily the true cast of the poet cannot be ignored. It is only that the unity of the poem and the unity of the poet's personality are interrelated. Various dispositions of the poet, such as character traits, abilities, psychology and the typology of these project in the poem. The degree and manner of projection of these psychic factors are, ofcourse dependent on the present state of literary structure.[3]

The writer's own experience and the thematic tradition of the national literature will influence her/his work. The recent trends in Indian writing in English and the general tradition of Indian Literature has certainly affected the poetic creativity of Kamala Das. The poetic experience in general is rooted in the individual poet's personal background as well as the regional and social factors. The mingling of this with the literary themes may result in a new thematic sphere.

Quite often some themes and motifs have to do with the writer's individuality and as a result they recur many times in such a writer. The motif of the pursuit of a lover occur/repeatedly in Kamala Das's poems. Many other motival terms such as "sun-stained", "Sun-scorched," "love-lorn," and the term related to cremation occur repeatedly. These motifs may have their source either in an experience which has had long lasting influence or they have to do with the mental state of the writer.

The artist's resistance to the social norms which is projected in the work results in a sort of "autostylization."[4] This is seen in Kamala Das's "The Freaks" (*Summer in Calcutta*) where the persona declares that she is a freak. This autostylization expresses the writer's negative attitude to the contemporary social reality. Kamala Das and those of the writers who think in this way thus practise "autostylization." However, the non-personal poems of Kamala Das establish relationship between herself and the society. This, therefore, offers a contrast.

The origin of personal experience is spatial. The space, the physical "here" has an originary status in most of the modern writers. It is from 'space' that subjects of sensory experience originate : the inorganic, the flora and fauna, human consciousness and even language have sprung from it. These are physically present realities. However poetry makes use not only of the physically present, but also of the absent which exists in time, in memory or only in the complex thought processes. The mythical and the wishful do not belong to space and therefore belong to the realm of the absent. Since a poet like Kamala Das quite often lapses into the realm of the absent while depicting present reality the dialectical interplay of presence and absence quite often occurs in the poems of poets like her.

Praising the unknown the poets call attention to the unknown experience, refreshing the reader's view through giving new dimensions to language. Things that spring from space are perishable, and hence the human experience springs from the perishable. Thus, the core of the imperishable poetry is the perishable phenomena. The physically present perishable human body, the source of energy and desire, is the originator of experience which is manifested in the form of poetry. Hence, the sensual poet describes with meticulous care various aspects of human body which is the source of energy and desire. The "limbs," "the plants," the sun in the mid-day sky with its energy spread out are all (in Kamala Das's poetry) objects expressing natural desire.

Natural desire, therefore, is the focus of the erotic/love poems. The syntax and lexis, the semantic and phonological aspects are the carries of this desire in poetry. The desire thus carried in is presence and it is aesthetically marked in poetry. In Kamala Das, the transfer from the celebration of love and lust to anxiety and frustration is the transfer from presence to absence — the manifestation of the absence of the reality sought for. However, in her poems dealing with finding satisfaction in an imaginary lover there is the dialectical interplay of presence and absence. When the attempts to attain fulfilment are met with defeat, this "defeat leads to the most meaningful kind of experience, that kind which deals with the intransigent aspects of our experience which fail to fit into our ways of perceiving the world, opening up a new terrain for us to explore and forcing out of preconceived views of experience and the world."[5] Kamala Das's "Woman without Her Shadow" presents such an experience.

The love poems of Kamala Das like "Love", "In Love" and "Ghanashyam" have their origin in the "presence" noted above, and the "absence" in them helps open up further "presence" by the impressions of the world which shapes a point of view. The battle between love and death (cf. "Substitute"), and the sun (cf. "In Love", "Summer in Calcutta") too is both presence and absence. The unity, the sun, thus signifies love and no love, life and death in terms of presence and absence. This would mean that images such as that of the 'sun' signify the undifferentiated nature of presence and absence suggesting the undifferential nature of human experience. Thus, the course that Kamala Das takes in her poems seems to be dialectical.

From the preceding discussion it is clear that this study of self and sensuality in Kamala Das's poetry deviates from the commonsensical notions of the literary critics. The force of Kamala Das's poems lies in their being able to transform the frustrating present which is marred by estrangement of the self from the other. However, this estrangement helps her by making her able to identify the totality of individual existence. In the poems that celebrate love and lust she attempts to convert the loss — that which is absent — into pure presence of joy. The love poems we have taken for analysis in this chapter are those that satisfy the need to fill the loneliness and help overcome suicidal impulse. For Kamala Das imagination carries the strength to reveal the passing brilliance of things in the surroundings. When she describes the real in her own terms with all its sensory qualities, the emotions that result carry in them her aesthetic evaluation of life as such . In order to fill the void resulting out of estrangement of the self from the world she uses the empathic energies of poetry.

The sexual exercises and the physical and mental exhaustion represented in her poems could be visualized as an endeavour to achieve self-identity through poetry. At the same time the readers of her poetry, and, the in fact the readers of all poetry, are aware that depicting life means depicting human experiences. Hence, all and only experience constitutes literature depicting life. Since literature in general and poetry in particular is mimesis, its content is emotional, intellectual or sensual experience. In presenting sensual experience, the rest of the experience are suspended. This single experience may not represent life in full since this deals with human relationship on the plane of sex experience. That sex is the origin of emotions like love, attachment, jealousy, hatred and frustration, makes it a factor determining the personality of the individual. Here we do not consider sex as an act of procreation. However, the representation of sex in poetry is not an easy task, because :

> The subject of sex, through one of the most important, is one of the most suppressed in a social set up. The inhibitive influence of society is felt to a much greater extent when the writer is concerned with sex theme as content than when he is concerned with any other theme...Thus by his choice of the sex theme as content, the writer is necessarily concerned with the expression of content as 'aesthetic fact' as well as 'social fact'.[6]

Sex experience becomes aesthetic material when it has any one or all of the correlates : the intellectual, emotional and sensual. Since what is aesthetic is artistic, artistic treatment of sex theme is aesthetic The content is the aesthetic material and the formal representation of the theme generates the aesthetic effect. A vulgar representation of sex, therefore, is not aesthetic. In a coherent piece of poem dealing with sex, obscenity evaporates and the residue is aesthetic experience. Moreover, through the organisation of the subject matter into an aesthetic whole, it is the pleasure of existence that is celebrated. The poet in such poems creates an inner world of his or her own which is shared by the reader and thus enables the reader also to celebrate the joy of being an individual. The formal features of the poem depict the truth — sex in its totality and allows the poet's as well as reader's mind concentrate on it and derive the desired goal in its capacity to excite the mind and make feel both the writer and the reader as individuals who exist in space and time. This sort of representation of reality is aesthetic and this underlines the approach to Kamala Das's poetry in this chapter.

On another plane representation of sexuality in poetry could be viewed, as Michel Foucault did, as the channel through which power and knowledge join together to penetrate and control the individual's private pleasures, desires and behaviour. Repression, prohibition, exclusion and domination are a part of the power relation existing in society. Foucault calls them negative mechanism of constraints. The system of marriage and development of kinship ties are "built around a system of rules defining the permitted and the forbidden, the licit and the illicit."[7] According to Foucault sexuality is "a great surface network in which stimulation of bodies, the intensification of pleasures, the incitement to discourse, the formation of special knowledges, the strengthening of controls and resistances, are linked to one another, in accordance with a few major strategies of knowledge and power."[8] Sexuality, apart from its connections with social norms of marriage and productivity is "addressed to the body, to the life, to what causes it to proliferate, to what reinforces the species, its stamina, its ability to dominate, or its capacity for being used."[9]

The structure of the poetic language which carries sensual pleasures will, when examined, reveal how pleasure is linguistically manifested. The device of metaphor is important in the manifestation of sex as the signifier of the female self — sex as the determinant of the woman's identity. This function of metaphors in sensual poetry by women as a determinant of female identity is the most significant role sexuality can play in the life of one who yearns for individuality, knowledge and pleasure. In the erotic poems of Kamala Das, the lexicon of sexual excitement such as "unending lust," "the pumps and the pipes," "breasts," "female hungers," operate as instances signalling mental and physical excitement, creating a sense of intense sensuality.

Such poems of Kamala Das develop sexual allusions and references of sexual encounters in the peculiar language of metaphors. Expressions like "pelvic thrust", "His body needing mine", "race towards love". "embrace," "mouth on mouth" are descriptions signifying sexual act from the peripheral to the central. The climax of such uses of lexicon is physical sexual encounter as evident in "In Love" *Summer in Calcutta* (SC) :

> ......When mouth on
> Mouth, I lie, ignoring my poor
> Moody mind, while pleasure
> With deliberate gaiety
> Trumpets harshly into the
> Silence of the room...

The lexical and syntactic incitement of sexuality, while pointing towards the definition of woman as the signifier of sex, is a determinant of the knowledge of selfhood for woman. Reading such sensual poems excites the pleasure faculty of the female reader and helps her realize her own identity as being. Sex, therefore, is a mode of knowing the self for women — the self discovery and self assertion are predicated on an endless "desire for sex." This desire underlies the need to experience sex, know it and possess it. Foucault has pointed out that this obsessive desire for sex is one of the "most essential internal operating procedures" which operates both on the poetic persona and the reader to generate the need that connects each to the production of sexualities.

Erotic energy, which is released in sexual encounters may be the factor that helps her to carry on the search for identity. If the poet mates with the Muse transcendence of beauty and passion occurs. If it is with the mythological 'bull' the result is pleasure. It is the latter that takes place in the case of Kamala Das. This means that she challenges the existing set up which demands self-abnagation which imposes loneliness. Kamala Das's protagonist found her relationship with her husband a suitable ground to project her own freedom as being. In the drama of her life with her husband she visualises herself as a victim of oppression, who is tempted to disobey the conventional life he represents. This vision of reality which is related to Kamala Das's aesthetics dominates her poems. Thus, in her poems one can see the male characters only in relation to her and not as separate individuals.

The 'aggressiveness' of the erotic poet is often covered with self doubt. When the sense of guilt is overcome, the self assurance seems to emerge, as is seen in the last few lines of "An Introduction" (SC) :

> It is I who laugh, it is I who make love
> And then feel shame, it is I who lie dying
> With a rattle in my throat. I am sinner,
> I am saint.. I have no joys which are not yours, no
> Aches which are not yours. I too call myself I.

In poems such as "Summer in Calcutta, "In Love", "The

Freaks'' and ''The Wild Bougainvillae'' although the speaker endeavours to convince herself of the presences, absences and transformations she sees in the burning sun and burning pyre, she feels that the world of objects and perceptions are separated by her own sensual approach. This awareness tempts her mind towards the desire to drown in sensuality (which is the main force in ''Summer in Calcutta'' (SC) :

> ....I drink and drink
> Again, I am drunk,
> Yes but on the gold
> Of suns. What noble
> Venom now flows through
> My Veins....

The release of erotic energy seems to be a necessary precondition of poetic creation in most of the poems in Kamala Das's first three volumes of poetry. Her persona's bondage to her husband was a fetter to her need to free her imagination, while the same has provided her with the urgency and emotional intensity noticeable in her poems. She declares that she cannot share with her husband the world as the ideal couple of the social system, or the mythical 'ardhanareswara' is believed to share. Kamala Das's persona, therefore, undertakes the search for pleasure and identity by herself, views every male physically near to her as an 'other'.

Since this is an attempt to study the formal features of poems by a woman writer, a note on the question of language use specific to woman is not out of place. The clues are drawn from a discussion on ''double binds'' by Eleanor Kuykendall.[10] The capacity to speak and write without being overtly aware of the rules that exist in the language is considered as the speaker's or user's capacity to organize thought. Linguists have often pointed out that women habitually use non assertive forms where assertive form is required to create the real impact. A sentence such as ''I think that perhaps what we want is to be strong women'' is characterised by the feminine non assertiveness showing the lack of force which the declarative sentence ''we want to be strong woman'' carries. In this example the assertive sentence ''we want to be strong women'' is transformed into indirect or non-assertive.

This is argued as non serious sentence in Robin Lackoff.[11] A serious sentence according to Lakoff is a sentence whose producer is perceived as unambivalent in intending to carry out the speech act (this is related to Searle's sincerity condition). According to Lakoff women are caught in a kind of linguistic dilemma requiring them to speak and write non-assertively in order to be perceived as women, but requiring them to speak and write assertively to be taken seriously. If a women makes a serious assertive utterance it would be inappropriate for her gender or she is not simply feminine in speech and writing. Thus, either way the woman is participating in her own rejection. The linguistic double binds the society has imposed on the woman thus infringe on her right to self expression.

The nuances in the women's language which Kuykendall notes as female markers have the following traits :

> Female markers cut across classification of what is usually considered to describe and explain linguistic structure — such as syntax, semantics, and phonology. Female markers include vocal transformations of declarative sentences into questions and hedges like "I think" and "perhaps" as well as changes in word order. They ascribe mental attitude — ambivalence in intent to assert — to speakers who alter declarative sentence by voice, word choice, or word order.[12]

When the women user of a language — be it Malayalam or English — realizes that the female markers in her speech or writing are inappropriate for delivery or insufficient to create the necessary impact — that it is nonassertive — she will recognize the contradiction in intention. This is the contradiction between the form of her utterance and its topic and content. This is what creates the ambivalence. The realization of her own ambivalence necessitates self-reflection and realizing the inappropriateness of the indirect assertion breaks the linguistic double bind.

Kamala Das has largely overcome this problem in her writing in Malayalam which is her mother tongue. Unlike other women writers of Malayalam she is assertive and unambivalent. Being a non-native user of English Kamala Das may choose to use the structure of English she has learned. Her knowledge of the English language should be the knowledge of the standard variety and the literary variety of the standard where grammaticality as well as deviation are the main concern. Moreover, her breaking of the double binds in the case of her mother tongue may be an incentive for her to avoid the non-assertive forms in English.

In what follows twenty selected poems (six hundred and nine lines) of Kamala Das are analysed. The analysis may be an alternative to the elusive critical concepts of climax, resolution and artistic unity. How the factors discussed so far are formally represented is the point of concern here. The text of the poem is given first and is followed by detailed examinations of various stylistic devices. Conclusions regarding the theme of each of the poems are drawn on the basis of the formal evidence. "An Introduction" (SC) which is often referred to as Kamala Das's 'manifesto' will receive attention first.

An Introduction

I don't know politics but I know the names
Of those in power, and can repeat them like
Days of week, or names of months, beginning with
Nehru. I am Indian, very brown, born in
Malabar, I speak three languages, write in
Two dream in one. Don't write in English, they said,
English is not your mother-tongue. Why not leave
Me alone, critics, friends, visiting cousins,
Every one of you? Why not let me speak in
Any language I like? The language I speak
Becomes mine, its distortions, its queernessess
All mine, mine alone. It is half English half
Indian, funny perhaps, but it is honest,
It is as human as I am human, don't
You see? It voices my joys, my longings, my
Hopes, and it is useful to me as cawings

17. Is to crows or roaring to the lions, it
18. Is human speech, the speech of the mind that is
19. Here and not there, a mind that sees and hears and.
20. Is aware. Not the deaf, blind speech
21. Of trees in storm or of monsoon clouds or of rain or the
22. In coherent mutterings of the blazing
23. Funeral pyre. I was child, and later they
24. Told me I grew, for I become tall, my limbs
25. Swelled and one or two places sprouted hair, when
26. I asked for love, not knowing what else to ask
27. For, he drew a youth of sixteen into the
28. Bedroom and closed the door. He did not beat me
29. But my sad woman-body felt so beaten.
30. The weight of my breasts and womb crushed me. I shrank
31. Pitifully. Then... I wore shirt and my
32. Brother's trousers, cut my hair short and ignored
33. My womanliness. Dress in sarees, be girl
34. Be wife, they said. Be embroiderer, be cook,
35. Be quareller with servants. Fit in. Oh,
36. Belong, cried the categorizers. Don't sit
37. On walls or peep through our lace-draped windows.
38. Be Amy, or be Kamala. Or, better
39. Still, be Madhavikutty. It is time to
40. Choose a name, a role. Don't play pretending games.
41. Don't play at schizophrenia or be a
42. Nympho. Don't cry embarassingly loud when
43. Jilted in love.... I met a man, loved him. Call
44. Him not by any name, he is every man
45. Who wants a woman, just as I am every

Woman who seeks love. In him... the hungry haste
Of rivers, in me... the oceans' tireless
Waiting. Who are you, I ask each and every one,
The answer is, it is I. Anywhere and,
Everywhere, I see the one who calls himself
I, in this world, he is tightly packed like the
Sword in its sheath. It is I who drink lonely
Drinks at twelve, midnight, in hotels of strange towns,
It is I who laugh, it is I who make love
And then feel shame, it is I who lie dying
With a rattle in my throat. I am sinner,
I am saint. I am the beloved and the
Betrayed. I have no joys which are not yours, no
Aches which are not yours. I too call myself I.

The title "An Introduction" and the placement of the first person pronoun "I" in the thematic position hint at the subject matter of the poem. What the poet might tell might have to do with herself. The poem as a whole is not separated into sections, but one can identify certain sections or segments in it. On the first reading the only instability that is noticeable in the world within the poem is the sudden shift in narration — five times, each representing an aspect of the theme. Despite this shift the poem has unity because the various aspects contained in each of the undistinguished segments in the poem are related to what the speaker says. The connection between these undistinguished segments and the speaker is maintained throughout the length of the poem. Thus, the use of first person 'I' in the following manner acts as a cohesive device : once in lines 4, 5, 14, 23, 26, 30, 31, 43, 45, 48, 49, 50, 51, 52, 55, 56, 58, twice in lines 1, 10, 24, 54, 57, 59. It is seen that towards the end of the poem the use of first person pronouns becomes more consistent, a sign of giving emphasis to the speaker's individuality. Matters of tense and time reference assume significance here. In the undistinguished first segment that ends in line four this is presented in a realistic vein. In these lines the speaker is referring to things perceived in the immediate present and she is associating as well as dissociating herself from a given situation — political — as preliminary to her attempt to isolate herself, and define as an individual who exists independently. The present tense runs into the second segment also where she talks about the language of her choice against odds. But in the third segment where the speaker is in a restrospective mood, the tense is shifted to the past simple. After the 16th line present tense is resumed only to give way to the past immediately. There is the interplay of past and present until line 48. The poem ends up in the assertions in present tense. The tense pattern and the use of first person pronoun hint at a significant aspect of Kamala Das's poetry — depiction of personal feelings in relation to time and space.

The world within the poem is no doubt constructed out of language. This world within the poem shall have some human situation developing in it. The linguistic details of the poem help the reader to view this world in all its actualities. However the understanding of the situations developing within this world depends upon the way inferences are drawn from the linguistic details of the text. Yet, the personal world of the poem is in reality a mimesis of the external actualities which the poet shares with the readers.

The specificity achieved through the use of noun phrases containing definite article — lines 10, 17, 18, 20, 22, 27, 28, 30, 36, 46, 47, 49, 51 and 57 show specificity of reference. This implies that in the poem the world of actualities is subordinate to personal feelings. These linguistic components exemplify not any particular situation but the life as such of the speaker. In this way the poem's linguistic network, while showing the speaker's perception of things, makes the readers perceive them : this is how the private experience of the speaker is made known to the perceiving reader.

The first two segments of the poem are related to the depiction of various aspects of personal life. The presentation is realistic and vivid; the persons, events and actions are interconnected through the syntactic structure of the line. There is no noticeable semantic ill-formedness which makes the language opaque : events and actions take place in time and space; the main clause subordinate clause relationship are in their usual order. The style therefore is transparent. What then is that makes the poem interesting from the point of view of stylistics?

The way Kamala Das places determiners and how she sequentially presents first person pronoun, the culmination of which is assertion of individuality, has already been observed. It was also noted that the shifts in focus within the poem is accompanied by alternation of present tense and past tense and their interplay. The final assertion, however, is done wholly in present tense. The subject matter of the poem is explicit, the poem has an identity of its own and this identity depicts the identity the speaker. The poet, in the poem, is giving a vivid description of her experiences and convictions.

In the first two segments, that is, till line 23, the style follows that of one to one discourse. The rapid shifts, that have been noted earlier, are paralleled by appropriate settings. The opening part of the poem should be treated as speech acts since there is a seeming one-to-one interaction. The speaker who is the poet herself addresses the readers as well as those who are there in the world within the poem (''critics'', ''friends,'' ''visiting cousins'' and the ''they'' who are identified as the categorizers). Lines 7-23 are a direct address to an audience — an audience whose absence enables the poet to freely ask questions, issue commands and make assertions and requests. In the poem one notices the speaker asking questions, making assertions and making comparison to give explanation to what she believes to be true. This seemingly dialogic pattern gives a picture of the predominant thought in the poem and hints at its aesthetic organization.

The 6th line of the poem has the forbidding clause ''Don't write in English.'' It is pointed out by the speaker as an infringement on her individuality. In lines 7-10 the speaker asks two questions which are true questions except for the absence of an immediately present audience. By making these utterances the speaker is questioning the infringement on her right as an individual to select the language of her choice as the medium of poetic communication. But how does she expect the questions to affect the absent audience? The questioner (who is the poet) immediately adds several details which explain her stand. However, these explanations come immediately after the questions and make clear the fact that the questioner does not require answer to her questions. Though it appears that the poet's addressees are placed in the role of informants and she herself in the role of one who needs information the actual intention is some what different. Here a repetition of the statements about a true question seems to be in order. Questions, except the rhetorical ones, presuppose the immediate presence of the hearer and the speaker should have the right to ask the particular question. The abruptness of the questions show that the questions are sincere and serious and are asked to those who are in some way known to her. The questions, therefore, need not be taken for mere begging for information, because they tell the hearers indirectly not to meddle with her affairs. This means that the statements that follow the questions are additional explanations of the knowledge already shared by the hearers. Thus, the poet might be 'implicating' a warning, which is objection to the attitude of the people around her.

The underlying aspect of all the five undistinguished segments in the poem is the description of the poet's experiences and convictions. The syntactic and semantic aspects of the foregoing leave no loophole for adverse criticism. The imagery effected in the comparisons in lines 16 to 23 is wide and varied : the frail crow, the mighty lion, the strong wind, the cloud and rain and the blazing funeral pyre form part of the range of imagery. All these suggest the turbulence in the speaker's mind while she puts questions and makes assertions.

The third segment which begins with line 23 marks a shift in thought through shift into the temporal sequence of growth, maturity and aftermath. The temporal sequence bringing growth and change is presented in direct syntactic order.

> I was child
> I grew
> I became tall
> My limbs swelled
> I asked for love
> I shrank pitifully
> I wore a shirt and my brother's trousers

(I) cut my hair short and ignored my womanliness.

The direct syntactic order of these statements reflects the directness and realism of the speaker. These unambiguous statements make her intention explicit : she is speaking about the purely personal aspects of her life. Further the various stages of physical and mental development and the directionality of life towards the present state is also suggested in the direct presentation of temporal events. The society's objection to the rebellious attitude of the poet is given in imperative syntax :

Dress in sarees
Be girl
Be wife
Be embroiderer
Be cook
Be quarreller with servants

The elision of the subject 'you' while achieving brevity adds to the force of the strings : they have the effect of a sword. But soon this effect is counterbalanced by the use of the interjection : "Oh" : "Fit in, Oh/Belong, cried the categorizers", The interjection "Oh" is recorded as an "exclamation of surprise, fear etc." in the *Advanced Learner's Dictionary of Current English.* Further the term "cry" is a sign of lament. Hence, the force of the imperatives is lost in these two lines. However, the imperatives run on again :

...Don't sit
On walls or peep through our lace-draped windows.
Be Amy, or be Kamala. Or better
Still, be Madhavikutty. It is time to
Choose a name, a role. Don't play pretending games.
Don't play a Schizhophrenia or be a
Nimpho...

All these strings are commands : the sentences have no subjects and the verbs are in the imperative mood. The imperative is usually contrasted with the statements, questions and exclamations. While revealing the society's opinion of her, these imperatives build a syntactically as well as semantically contrasting atmosphere which mimes the conflict that she has been facing. The illocutionary force of these imperatives is inapparent in that they had been uttered in the past and are being reported by the speaker. Since they had been uttered in the past, the reason why she is reproducing them here might be to exemplify some of her thoughts regarding herself which the imperatives help explain. The purpose served by this style would become further clear when the context in which the speech acts appear is subjected to an examination.

Earlier it was said that the speaker in the poem is attempting to identify her own unique position through asserting her right to speak, write and select a male companion. The so called categorizers are there to offer a contrast to the speaker's assertions as a free individual. The contrast therefore yields what seems to be the preference of the speaker. Her stand will become further clear when the last segment is looked at from near.

The use of present tense and dynamic verbs — verbs that suggest activity, process and bodily sensations — in the closing segment of the poem convey the emotions of the pleasure seeking individual and the woman's perception of the male ego : thus, the thoughts discernible in the opening lines culminates in the aggressive assertion of individuality. The lines in a way define the male view of himself and of his view of the women which the poet cannot approve of :

> Anywhere and,
> Everywhere, I see the one who calls himself
> I; in this world, he is tightly packed like the
> Sword in its sheath.

The male tendency to view himself as unique and to subordinate the female as a mere medium for pleasure is thwarted in this part of the poem. The female speaker feels herself equal or even "more equal" in the act of pleasure defining individuality.

The rapidity with which images appear from line 52 onwards suggests the urgency of the poet's purpose. The seeming dissolution of the self in several masks ("sinner," "saint," "beloved," "betrayed") along with the self-imposed estrangement results in the assertion of individuality : the dissolution is only on the surface. The first two masks- "saint" and "sinner"— evoke antithetical, yet co-present states of mind. When the speaker assumes the guise of the beloved and the betrayed simultaneously, the same is the effect. However, the saint and the sinner are physically and psychologically separated from the twin mask of the beloved and the betrayed. Thus, the poet dramatises the self's need to define itself, to provide an identity.

O.N.V. Kurup, who sees "naked beauty of truth" in the *Summer in Calcutta* poems, distinguishes "An Introduction" by calling it "an autobiography epitomised in a few words."[13] Linda Anderson, in her essay on the psycho-analytic approach to self says that "it is necessary to take into account the fact that the woman who attempts to write herself is engaged by the nature of activity itself in rewriting the stories that already exist about her since by seeking to publicise herself she is violating an important cultural construction of her feminity as passive or hidden."[14] By exposing the details about her the woman writer is resisting or changing what is known about her. The search for identity by the woman writer is explained in the following way :

> The myth of self which recent theorists have questioned may not be present for her in the same way; it is more difficult for her to believe in a self that can exist before writing, a self that is unified and continuous. Autobiography may self-consciously exist for her : an alternate place for identification. This means that there may be a greater formal awareness in her writing, an emphasis on the self-reflexiveness of writing, the idea of the self as written.[15]

The act of self-naming and the emphatic declaration "I too call myself I" make the act of assertion of individuality which gradually develops from the first segment of the poem complete.

The foregoing discussion may serve as an introduction to the stylistic strategy of Kamala Das. In the following pages the language of the love poems is examined and it is shown how the poet's search for individuality and her aesthetics of sensuality go hand in hand. In the discussion that immediately follows ("Love"-SC) Kamala Das's handling of the love theme in a soft vein is examined. This will lead to those love poems where her language is "aggressively individualistic."

Love

1. Until I found you,
2. I wrote verse, drew pictures,
3. and, went out with friends
4. For walks...

5. Now that I love you,
6. Curled like an old mongrel
7. My life lies, content
8. In you...

The poem is very short : it has only 32 words. This poem which rejects conventional poetic form and which has minimal poetic structure is a characteristic piece exhibiting the latest trends in Indian poetry in English. Before the analysis begins something has to be said about the poetic structure.

The linguistic structure of a poem is characterized mainly by repetition within. Except this, poetry has no special linguistic structure of its own. This is substantiated in Roman Jakobson's statement that the poetic function is the set towards message as such (Cf. Chapter Two, discussion on Roman Jakobson). However, poetic language is, characteristically, in conflict with the structure of language. In traditional poetry lines are sentence-like units. But this is not so in modern poetry. If we take the lines of Kamala Das's verse as sentence-like units, then enjambment[16] might be seen causing mismatch of sentence and verse line.

Apart from the deep structure and surface structure which standard language and poetic language share, the poetic language has the distinguishing poetic structure.[17]

The interplay of poetic constraints and surface structure variation presents the deep structure of the poem. A good poem will show variation of deep structure and will be accompanied by a minimum variation of surface structure and poetic sturcture.[18] This observation might be of use in the study of Kamala Das's "Love". It could be intuitively understood that the poem is a typical piece of mesial poetry treating the theme of love. This intuitive judgement could be elaborated and explained by examining the interplay of deep structure and poetic structure and the intelligent use of the tenses.

Time in the first stanza is past definite. But there is no direct statement about the space; the location where the things happen is unspecified. Here all the events are temporal. In the second stanza too there is only a vague presence of the spatial element. The comparison of the abstraction "life" with the concrete "mongrel" is the only spatial image in the poem. However, in effect this too is temporal, because what is spatial in it is insignificant to the message. The apparent lack of importance of space gives prominence to the temporal aspects, thereby suggesting that the love depicted in the poem is not ephemeral. The "I" and "you" relationship is depicted with reference only to time, thereby giving it a touch of sublimeness. This shows that in this poem the poet's attitude is not aggressive.

The first stanza does not show Deep Structure violation. However its violation in the second stanza is significant; the result of the violation is an apt image. The main Surface Structure variation too is in the second stanza, that is, the adjunct "curled like an old mongrel" is preposed. This is the poet's response to the pragmatic potential of the language — this evokes a sublime emotion.

In the first reading, the first stanza would appear like a sentence divided into the four lines. However, on close reading it would become clear that the stanza is an attention calling device, or a preface preparing the reader to meet the poeticality of the second stanza. Further this stanza helps juxtapose the second stanza with it to yield the desired output.

While the Poetic Structure and Surface Structure are undifferentiated in the first stanza, they are undifferentiated through mismatch in the second stanza. The ill-formed Deep Structure and Surface Structure of the second stanza convey the poem's message. Thus, the effect of the violation has to do with human characteristics — the life of one person lying curled in another in perfect contentment, forgetting the limits imposd by space. This externalises the inalienable nature of pure love, which is beyond space and hence beyond the limitations of body.

The above analysis provides some sort of counterpoint to what follow. If the love depicted in the poem "Love" transcends body, it is the carnal hungers of the body that find expression in poems like "In Love". In "In Love" the search for identity and pleasure seems to go hand in hand. Before starting the analysis of such a piece a consideration of certain shades of eroticism seems to be in order.

The Indian conception of spirituality, the four *Purusharthas* ("Dharma," "Artha," "Kama" and "Moksha"), has physical love, as one of its part. The pursuit of sexual pleasure is, therefore, a legitimate affair. The twelfth canto of Jayadeva's *Gita Govinda* describes the process of love making openly.[19] This work which inspired art for a long time is still a source of inspiration to poets. Amaru in his *Sataka* (popularly known as *Amarusataka*) introduces various moods of physical love. He views "love" from an aesthestic angle, and his poetry is astir with "the quivering music of long vowels and liquid consonants."[20] Amaru describes human body in its full beauty when violent passion rules it. He portrays the emotional intensity of the lovers as effectively as may make the reader enter the world within it. Bhartrhari's *Srngarasataka* has a section entitled "Sambhogavarnana" (description of dalliance). A translation of stanza 31 of this work is quoted below to offer an example of the description of beauty in Indian tradition :

> In this world there is the stigma and shame of having to serve a tyrannical king for a livelihood; how could a self-respecting man preserve his pride and fortitude if there were not this lotus eyed who store the rising moon beams in their frames, dangle lovely waistbands and have shapely breasts and waists.[21]

These are some of the dominant approaches to "love" in the Indian tradition. Not to mention various other schools of aesthetics that treat similar theme that offer background to an Indian writer who seeks to express in verse his or her own quest for love. Kamala Das's love poems, however, have an additional factor — the quest for identity. It has been observed how seriously she argues for her own individual right in "An Introduction". "In Love" (SC) is a poem that contains the poet's 'aggressive' quest for pleasure and identity.

In Love

Of what does the burning mouth
Of sun, burning in today's
Sky remind me... oh, yes, his
Mouth, and... his limbs like pale and
Carnivorous plants reaching
Out for me, and the sad lie
Of my unending lust. Where
Is room, excuse or even
Need for love, for, isn't each
Embrace a complete thing, a
Finished jigsaw, when mouth on
Mouth, I lie, ignoring my poor
Moody mind, while pleasure
With deliberate gaiety
Trumpets harshly into the
Silence of the room.. At noon
I watch the sleek crows flying
Like poison on wings — and at
Night, from behind the Burdwan
Road, the corpse-bearers cry 'Bol
Hari Bol', a strange lacing
For moonless nights, while I walk
The verandah sleepless, a
Million questions awake in
Me, and all about him, and
This skin-communicated
Thing that I dare not yet in
His presence call our love.

As in the case of erotic poems in general the thoughts this poem expresses are simple. The theme is sexual love and associated feelings. Though the theme needs not much explication, the subtlety of Kamala Das's treatment of love which is visible in the various passing emotional phases is one that catches the literary analyst's attention.

The speaker in the poem is in a reflective mood : she reflects on an ecstatic union with her lover and then evaluates its impact on her. The poem is not divided into stanzas. There is no striking deviance of grammatical restrictions. Nor are there any phonological or typographical variations. The word order, with a few exceptions is almost direct prose order. However, the formal structures in the poem convey with intensity, the desire, the actions and the doubts of the speaker.

The poem begins with an expression of burning passion : the burning sun reminds the speaker of her amours with the lover. Kamala Das juxtaposes words in order to present iconically the juxtaposition of the partners in coitus. This is effected through the phrase "mouth on mouth" in lines eleven-twelve. The encounter as such is explained by the choice of syntax. In the following lines the syntactic inversion locates the position and movement of the bodies :

> ...his limbs like pale and
> Carnivorous plants reaching
> Out for me, and the sad lie
> Of my unending lust...

The direct word order of the first three lines in the above is achieved by preposing the verbal "reaching out for me". The reordered version thus gives the position and movement of the body : "his limbs reaching out for me like pale and carnivorous plants." Kamala Das's use of inversion is to indicate spatial inversion, showing the speaker's position in the sex act. The effect of this upon an average reader is neither attraction nor repulsion but excitement which is accompanied by bewilderment. This, precisely, is what Kamala Das intends to achieve by the use of such formal devices.

Kamala Das makes intelligent use of the syntax to present the tempo of the physical movement in lines 10-16. The syntax enacts the movements of the bodies while coitus is progressing with remarkable vigour. Continuity of this action is effected through the succession of syntactic units which begin with "where is room..." and end with "Trumpets harshly into the/Silence of the room..." Kamala Das carefully controls the movement of the syntax so that it mimes the action in progress — using a long flowing structure to denote the rhythmic movement of the bodies and breaking with syntactic break (ellipsis) at the climax, leaving the rest for the reader to guess :

> ...while pleasure
> With deliberate gaiety
> Trumpets harshly into the
> Silence of the room...

The asyndetic structures[22] iconically convey simultaneous movement[23] and in this way the active participation of the speaker is iconically presented in lines ten to sixteen. After the act, to present the consecutive images suggesting disparate experience which causes dullness and doubt, the poet uses polysyndetic structures.[24] The overall impact of these upon the reader produces in him a feeling akin to the one the speaker builds up for herself.

Another significant formal feature of the poem contributing to its meaning is the radical variation discernible in the texture of its syntax. This variation is in consonance with the need to give the emotional information to the reader. Needless to say the syntax depicts the wild sensual atmosphere determined by the spatio-temporal correlates.

In line 16 Kamala Das returns to the process of recollection. This is followed by consecutive imagery of doubt. The sleek crows at mid-day, the night, the corpse bears and their cries of "Bol/Hari Bol" are images producing strange effect, perhaps indicative of the aftermath of the vigorous sex act. Thus, the poet juxtaposes two disparate states : one of utmost sensuality and the other of doubt and nullity.

From line 17 to the last the verse creeps with resounding phrases depicting delicate emotions through conjointed phrases — the co-ordinator 'and' appears once in line 18 and twice in line 25. The conjointed phrases due to their increasing and decreasing and then increasing structural weight produce the syntactic orchestration that heightens the feelings. The lines beginning with "At noon..." (Lines 17 to 28) have temporal features (Cf. "noon" and "at night") in the beginning. Then they degenerate into a direct object ("him") — only to rise to the complex sentence with which the poem ends. Thus, the movement of syntax imitates rising-falling-rising rhythm. Taken together these rhythmic changes convey the emotional conflict between wild ecstacy and feelings of doubt and dullness. Thus, from sensuality the poet lapses into self analysis. If there is coherence in the sexual union, it is the opposite that the speaker in the poem experiences after that. The feeling of ephemerality and the angst, thus, prepares ground for the search for individual freedom.

A subjective poet like Kamala Das may not often mingle angst and protest with sensuality. Often a celebration of sensuality alone is a mark of her approach to life. In such poems lust may remain under the surface of visual and other sorts of pleasures. Below, the title piece of her first volume, wherein is discernible lust in dissolved state, is taken up for analysis.

Summer in Calcutta

1. What is this drink but
2. The April sun, squeezed
3. Like an orange in
4. My glass? I sip the
5. Fire, I drink and drink
6. Again, I am drunk
7. Yes, but on the gold
8. Of suns. What noble
9. Venom now flows through
10. My veins and fills my
11. Mind with unhurried
12. Laughter? My worries
13. Doze. Wee bubbles ring
14. My glass, like a bride's
15. Nervous smile, and meet

16. My lips. Dear, forgive
17. This moment's lull in
18. Wanting you, the blur
19. In memory. How
20. Brief the term of my
21. Devotion, how brief
22. Your reign when I with
23. Glass i hand, drink,
24. And drink again this
25. Juice of April suns.

The poem begins with the ratiocinative question "What is this drink but/The April sun, squeezed/Like an orange in/My glass? The question is addressed to the speaker herself. This sort of question throws light on the emotions and thoughts of the speaker — it is usually a feature of dramatic monologue and of poetry written in the form of conversation.

The emotion in "Summer in Calcutta" is closely linked with sensory experiences. The sensuality of the experience and its connection with the emotional state of the speaker is constructed linguistically through the interaction of concrete and abstract terms.

The concrete term *Calcutta* and the abstract term *Summer* with which the title is constituted do not in themselves specify a time, place or identity. "Summer" denotes time's general seasonal function. The term "Calcutta" has nothing particular to do with the Indian city called Calcutta. They are only components that help the presentation of a highly sensuous experience.

Experience is abstract mental process while its cause could be concrete individual object. The "orange" which appears in line 3 is a concrete specifier of an abstract experience — passing from the object "orange" we find abstracting and generalising in thinking about orange. If we look at the sun and an orange simultaneously we do not think of abstractions but see two objects. When Kamala Das draws a comparison between the April sun and an orange, she is simultaneously presenting two images : one the sun in the sky which is real and the other which is not near at hand and therefore an object which is absent. The sun reminding the poet of an orange itself stands for many condensed sensations. In condensation, according to Freud, lie in condensed state, in quite simple and clear statements, hidden meanings which could not be analysed by means of other literary methods.[25] The work of displacement serves to conceal the content of thoughts by displacing emphasis from the important to the trivial — from the sun to the orange — where in this context serves as a sex symbol holding key to the truth that man is the symbolic animal and that the creation of symbols is a fundamental activity of the sound mind. While most symbols are sexual their role extends to the deepest aspects of experience — all symbols represent ideas of the self or of the phenomena of birth, copulation and death.[26] Further the use of the simile, that is, the April sun likened to an orange, supports the identification of different ideas "in terms of a pleasure-pain principle exemplified by the savage mind that only notices similarities which are easier to see (less painful) than differences."[27]

The linguistic parallel to the mental reduction of many sensations into a single event is the phrasal device of reducing it into a single syntactical construction, in this case an orange. The orange carries with its concreteness the aspect of abstraction one ("an") — sensations condensed into a single unit. Hence, in poetry the concrete is almost always there with the abstract as if its presence in this way is quite natural. This is what helps us understand the way the poet amalgamates her sensations and perceptions with the poem's structure.

John Milstead states that the poem itself constitutes one of the most important contexts for determining meaning because metaphor to a large degree is brought into being by the literary work itself. If a poetic statement consists in the merging or confrontation of different contexts then using only the semantic feature restrictions + concrete and – concrete we have the following possibilities for contextual crossover : (+concrete) + (+concrete), (+concrete) + (–concrete), and (–concrete) + (–concrete).[28] According to Milstead "a poem is a verbally formalised selective influence on the percepts and concepts in the reader's mind, from which arise the complex interaction of concrete and abstract, the images and relationships, which acts with time, place and circumstance of literary realization."[29] Poetry is visual thought and it is the complex interaction of the concrete and the abstract that generates the experience the poem contains.

It was shown that the sentence in the opening lines is a ratiocinative question. But apart from that lies the poeticality of the four lines : they contain a powerful image. Let us look at the lines once again.

> What is this drink but
> The April sun, squeezed
> Like an orange in
> My glass?

It is generally the presence of the concrete words that gives a poem its sensuous quality. However, the wholeness of the imagery in the lines quoted above is not wholly due to the concrete words "sun", "orange" and "glass." "April" and "my" are abstractions necessary to the total realization of the image. As a matter of fact "April" does not refer to the sun as a star but to an idea of the sun that is realized only in the this context through the modifier. Further the claim that the April sun is a drink is constructed with the following components :

"drink" which is + concrete and + human

"sun" which is + concrete and - human and this helps the reader visualize the image in its wholeness and fullness of sensuality. The word "my" which is the agent of interaction signals human presence. The descriptions are presented in relation to this human agent. This necessitates an explanation to both the descriptors : the abstract descriptor (stylistic) is one that "makes or perceives something abstract" and the concrete descriptor (stylistic) is one that "makes or perceives something concrete."[30] The agent, therefore, should be a part of the statement of concreteness or abstraction. The sensations of the agent are converted into language by the agent's (his or her) mind. The words in the poem are the result of the choice of the writer which in turn is controlled by a synthesis of ideas performed in his/her mind. This synthesis is in a way the product of interaction between sensation created by the sight of any object and the mind as such. Thus the human presence is of supreme importance in the poetry of the mode we have taken for study — the human agent is the perceiver and the narrator.

In "Summer in Calcutta," therefore, the human agent — the speaker — is the centre of interaction of linguistic elements. The way the concrete terms interact with the abstract in the first twelve lines of the poem is shown :

```
                    +C
What is this drink but
                     +h

     -C       +C       +C
The April sun, squeezed,
     -h       -h       +h

              +C
Like an orange in
              -h

-C  +C        -C+C
My glass? I Sip the
+h  -h        +h+h

+C -C+C                +C
Fire I drink and drink
-h   +h+h              +h

       -C      +C
Again, I am drunk
       +h      +h

                  +C
Yes, but on the gold
                   -h

     +C          -C
Of suns. What noble
     -h          +h

     +C       +C
Venom now flows through
     -h       -h
```

–C +C +C –C
My veins and fills my
+h
+h +h +h
–C –C
Mind with unhurried
+h –h
–C
Laughter?
+h

The concrete terms (+concrete) "drink," "sun", "squeezed," "Orange," "glass," "sip", "fire," "drink," "suns," "venom," "flows," "veins" and "fills" interact with abstract terms (-concrete) "April," "my," "I," "noble," "my, " my " mind," "unhurried" and "laughter" producing a luxuriant sensuous atmosphere. These semantic feature restrictions (+ -concrete and + -human) give a vivid picture of the texture of the concrete and abstract, with the human agent as the fulcrum. The poet's mind is thus seen to hover above a variety of sensations, and she presents a good many of them before the reader in a form that most adequately carries sensuousness.

The rest of the poem comprises imagery adequate to carry on the atmosphere created in the first twelve lines to a heightening of the sensuality through a suggestion to the speaker's lasciviousness : wee bubbles bubbling like the young bride's vibrant smile and perhaps the speaker's lips too vibrate in ecstacy. This feeling is dominating her lust. Hence, one doesn't fail to see the sensuousness created by the linguistic layout discussed in the preceding sections; lust is dissolved in the 'juice' she drinks. The atmosphere constructed thus shows that Kamala Das is a thorough investigator of all the sensuous feelings that a woman's mind is capable of experiencing. This approach of her's is visible (in a different shape) in "The Looking Glass" (*Descendants*).

The Looking Glass

1. Getting a man to love you is easy
2. Only be honest about your wants as

3. Women. Stand nude before the glass with him
4. So that he sees himself the stronger one
5. And believes it so, and you so much more
6. Softer, younger, lovelier... Admit your
7. Admiration. Notice the perfection
8. Of his limbs, his eyes reddening under
9. Shower, the shy walk across the bathroom floor,
10. Dropping towels, and the jerky way he
11. Urinates. All the fond details that make
12. Him male and your only man. Gift him all,
13. Gift him what makes you woman, the scent of
14. Long hair, the musk of sweat between the breasts,
15. The warm shock of menstrual blood, and all your
16. Endless female hungers. Oh yes, getting
17. A man to love is easy, but living
18. Without him afterward may have to be
19. Faced. A living without life when you move
20. Around, meeting strangers, with your eyes that
21. Gave up their search, with ears that hear only
22. His last voice calling out your name and your
23. Body which once under his touch had gleamed
24. Like burnished brass, now drab and destitute.

In this poem the author in *propria persona* gives directions to fellow women in the light of her own experiences. The speaker apparently tells a supposed audience of women about the 'aggressive' course of actions to be taken by any woman who wants to derive satisfaction out of her own body. The speaker tells her audience that fullness is achieved only when a woman makes maximum use of her sex potentials. However, she warns her audience that the eventualities of such course of actions shall have to be faced. Once again, it is the way Kamala Das manipulates the linguistic resources that gives the poem its worth.

The well chosen diction of the first sixteen lines with all the imperative and affirmative verbs carry the full force of the poem. In the last eight lines this force is not maintained. Therefore, it appears that the imperatives are not intended to show the speaker's need to assert herself before the imaginary addressees. However, they show the speaker's strength as an individual. They are, in a way, indicative of her approach to life — women should derive satisfaction out of their sexuality, challenging social norms. This could be through watching the naked male body, standing nude with him or enjoying all that the male body offers for pleasure. Hence Kamala Das's speaker seems to mean that the women should endeavour to know herself through sexual union.

In the first sixteen lines the speaker gives directions to fellow women. It could be understood intuitively that the women audience will be thrilled to receive such bold directions from a fellow woman. Despite this the reader might sense (intuitively) that these imperatives fail to satisfy at least two rules that constitute the speech act of ordering : that there is no immediately present audience and the speaker has not the power to issue directions. On proceeding further, it becomes clear that these directions are not commands. They express the thoughts of the speaker — thoughts about her own conception of love and aftermath. What is behind these imperatives and assertions, should, in such case, be an intent to project her own vision of an erotic life and what it would lead to.

Much of what Kamala Das's speaker says originates from the tension between the dynamic imperative language of the poem and the revealing of her own thoughts. The speaker's introductory statement is abrupt : it is about love. Here the term "love" is used as a stative verb denoting an abstraction. But in between lines 3 and 16 she uses dynamic verbs to demonstrate how the abstract could be realized through concrete means. While in uttering line 3 the speaker is asking the listeners to drill according to her directions, that is, to stand nude with a man and observe his nakedness, in lines 4, 5 and 6 she explains the various details of the male body to be watched and enjoyed. Then she affects a comparison between the male and the female bringing about the aspects that make them unique in their own way. The only male attribute is physical strength while the female is given three, namely, softness, tenderness and loveliness, all of them traditional attributes.

Line 6 sets off a series of imperatives which are commands, though they are not true commands from the view point of the speech act theory. Yet, within the world of the poem the poet is free to assert or command anything. But to what effect? The effect is implied in the series of actions she asks her audience to perform. And What are those actions to be performed? The answer may be obtained on examining the nature of the verbs. Line 3 has ‘‘stand’’, line six ‘‘admit,’’ line 7 ‘‘notice’’, lines 12 and 13 ‘‘gift’’ (this must be ‘‘give’’; for a consideration of the grammaticality of this part, see Bruce King 155). The objects of these verbs describe the naked bodies of the partners in sex, the physiological processes of their sex organs and finally the abstraction ‘‘lust’’. However, by these imperatives she is really ‘‘implicating’’ the production of pleasure. Lines 15 and 16 mark an end to the details of things to be done with the male partner : ‘‘(Gift him) all your endless female hungers.’’ In line 15 the speaker gives a shock to the reader ‘‘The warm shock of menstrual blood....’’ is really ‘shocking’ and in this is implied the aggressive potential of Kamala Das's verse.

The, implications are, however, counterbalanced in lines 17-24, where the speaker speaks about the absence of the lover. Here the loss suffered by the poet is expressed in imagistic terms. The women shall have to live without a lover, or even without love. Here Kamala Das explains the transcient nature of sexual love. It is a prediction and without this the poem would have lost its appeal.

The reader of the poem feels various shifts in mood as he reads : the poem shifts from statements to directions and then to prediction. These shifts add to the sensuosity of the poem by way of presenting visual and abstract images. The abstract images of the poem's end point to the awareness that activities of the sort described in the beginning may lead to estrangement which is at the same life's tragedy and triumph.

That the emotions carried by Kamala Das's poetic language are wide and varied supports the observation that she is good at the art of celebrating her own existence. However, as shown elsewhere, expression of disgust and angst is a trait discernible in an individual who seeks to liberate herself from the norms set by others. This is apparent in the linguistic structure of "The Corridors" (SC).

The Corridors

Why do I so often dream
Of a house where each silent
Corridor leads me to warm
Yellow rooms — and, loud voices
Welcome me, and rich, friendly
Laughter, and upturned faces,
Familiar, but I do
Not seem to recollect names
Or the real nature of their
Relationship with me?
Why do I remain ever
A stranger, tramping the lost
Lanes of a blinded mind, while
All around they recognise,
They love.. and, once aware, I
See the bed from which my love
Has fled, the empty room, the
Naked walls, count on fingers
My very few friends, and try
Helplessly to remember
Their faces or the words they
Used to make a moment or
Two such blessed, blessed gifts?
Why do I so often in
Dreams linger at strange doorways,
Lonely to the bone, feeling
Like an imposter, watching

28. The crowd who welcome me-and
29. Know, deep inside, the truth that
30. They know me by another
31. Name-a well-loved name I am
32. Powerless to recollect?

On the very first reading itself the impression is that the poem's focus is diffuse. An internal discourse of the poet which is not said in direct language becomes clear on a closer examination. As in the case of the majority of Kamala Das's poems discussed in this chapter, the subject matter is the search for existential freedom.

The poem comprises three questions spread in thirty two lines. Therefore, the analysis must begin with a consideration of what questions are. For an attempt of this sort we must turn to J.R. Searle and H.P. Grice (Cf. Chapter two of this book).

The illocutionary force of any utterance depends upon the use of the utterance; the purpose of the locution is met only if its constitutive conditions are satisfied. True questions, as opposed to rhetorical or examination questions, have different constitutive conditions. Searle lays down the following four conditions (which are related to Grice's Maxim of Quality) for a question to be true :

(i) The questioner does not have the information necessary to complete proposition truly; (ii) It is not obvious to the questioner and his audience that the audience will provide the information without being asked; (iii) the questioner wants the information; (iv) the question counts as an attempt to elicit information.[31]

The first question that runs into ten lines ("why do I so often dream... Relationship with me?") is not a true question because : (a) there is no physically present audience; (b) the speaker may know the answer to the question while the audience (the readers) may not, thus violating Searle's condition (ii); (c) it is in doubt whether the questioner wants the information sought or not. However literary questions generally violate conditions (ii) and (iv) and thus fail to be true questions. In this vein all the three questions with which the entire poem is constituted lack illocutionary force.

Although the three questions lack illocutionary force, it could be argued that in literature, especially in poetry, this loss is not real loss. Hence the violation of Searle's laws of asking questions results in the establishment of a limited situation — a personal situation — where the question is a mimesis. Hence the reader to whom the questions are supposedly asked need not give a reply, he need only be an audience or an observer to what the poet speaks. Within the world created in the poem the poet freely asks questions and issues commands to which the reader is only a witness and not an interlocutor who participates in the speech event. The reader is neither expected to answer the poet's questions, nor obey him nor believe his assertions in any literal sense. Yet it is apparent that within the world of the poem the questions are somehow answered and the commands are somehow obeyed.

Illocutionary force of a given utterance is determined clearly only in consultation with both linguistic and extralinguistic context. However the presence of certain syntactic elements within the question which as is the rule should not be part of a question will cause the destruction of its impact. These elements are called non-restrictive modifiers. There are a number of them in this poem of questions. So it seems appropriate to have a glance at the role of non-restrictive modifiers (NRMS) in a poem.

Edmund L. Epstein in his study of the role of non-restrictive modifiers in poetry[32] argues that they act as a "poetizing" influence on the text. He identifies the following four characteristics of non-restrictive modifiers :

(a) They are 'poetizers'

(b) They are emotional, even sentimental in character; that is, they strongly bear effect; and

(c) They are in some ways gratuitous for the sense, and may be 'discarded without serious injury.'

(d) Pronominal NRMS which could be called 'arhythmic modifiers,' bear more affect than modifiers in predicate position in separate sentences, from meaning-equivalent discourses.[33]

The explanation of (c) above shows that if we employ linguistic restriction we shall have to explain, or the reader may add his own explanation to what is there in the text. Thus, if the writer does observe the Gricean Maxim of Relation — Be Relevant — the poetic function will be absent. It is the breaking of the maxim that adds meaning other than what is actually said.

When Kamala Das speaks about the silence of the corridors leading to the warm and yellow rooms, she seems to be in a thought the following NRMS embody : "silent," "warm", "yellow", "loud", "rich", "friendly", "upturned", "real", "lost", "blessed," "empty", "naked", "count-on". "helplessly", "blinded", "strange", "deep", "well-loved".

These NRMS are embeded in the three questions. However, the attribution represented by the NRMS is not the sole illocutionary function of these three sentences.

The attribution represented by the NRMS has a self informative quality. True questions, in normal conditions, is not supported by this quality. Questions, especially true questions, confer ignorance. They show the need for information from outside. The question points at the meaning revealing future which solves puzzles. As against this, the 'attributives' refer to the past in which the evidence for the attribution has been obtained. Hence the attributives, which are the NRMS embeded in the three questions of the poem, modify and mitigate the questions. In effect they pull back the future force of the questions. As noted in the beginning of this analysis, the poem's focus is diffuse. It is the introduction of these NRMS that has given rise to the feeling of diffuseness and lack of proper focus. The NRMS and the questions in which they are embeded show that the speaker in the poem is lingering in the present and past and is at the same time striving to affect future. This expresses the dilemma of the estranged speaker. The speaker is seen to substitute the desolation of her present with the dreams which themselves signify the absent. The incompatibility of reality and the search for sexual fulfilment is presented in a diffused manner. The present is disgusting, the past, though not altogether bad, was not wholesome. The only hope therefore is the absent future to which the questions point.

The theme of the erotic poems in general is the search for sexual pleasure by men. In Kamala Das's erotic poems the order is reversed; it is the woman who searches male partners and complains about the futility of the affair after the encounter. This indicates that the attitude of the poet towards men is similar to the attitude of men in general towards women. While this attitude is an aspect of the male behaviour, in the poet it is a means to uphold her own rights. Such a theme is brilliantly converted into the language of art in "The Freaks" (SC).

The Freaks

He talks, turning a sun-stained
Cheek to me, his mouth, a dark
Cavern, where stalactites of
Uneven teeth gleam, his right
Hand on my knee, while our minds
Are willed to race towards love;
But, they only wander, tripping
Idly over puddles of
Desire... Can this man with
Nimble finger-tips unleash
Nothing more alive than the
Skin's lazy hungers? Who can
Help us who have lived so long
And have failed in love? The heart,
An empty cistern, waiting
Through long hours, fills itself
With coiling snakes of silence...
I am a freek. It's only
To save my face, I flaunt, at
Times, a grand, flamboyant lust.

In this poem the poet juxtaposes her persona's inner feelings and outer experiences to show that she is unique in her own way. Hence, Kamala Das is seen ignoring definitions in order to find a definition for herself. In the twenty lines of the poem she presents this feeling with care.

The poem begins with the third person pronoun "he" : in

the first reading itself the overpresence of pronominal forms is observable. They appear in the following order :

Line	Pronominal form
1	he
2	me, his
4	his
5	my
7	they
13	us
18	I, it
19	I

The personal pronoun denoting a male — a man — is placed in the thematic position. The accusative "me " and the possessive "his" occur in line 2 and the first person "I" appears only in the 18th and 19th lines. Hence, the rate of presence and the placement of the pronominals and the appearance of the plural "us" in the 13th line suggest that the theme is essentially about relation between a man and the speaker. Within the poem's context the feminity is projected only through the capacity of the "I" to have coitus with the "he". That the relation between the persona represented by the first person pronoun "I" and the man represented by the third person pronoun "he" is sexual is suggested in the first line itself : the poem begins with physical details and actions of the man. The placement of "He talks" in the thematic position of a sentence that runs into almost half of the poem and the embedded NRMS giving physical details give the impression that the theme is restricted to man-woman relation.

The possessive his occurs twice, in *his mouth* and in *his right hand.* Here the speaker is describing the body of her sexual partner. It must be noted that these two phrases have something significant to say. Since "his" occurs only in these two phrases, there does not seem to be an explicit implication that both the parts (*his mouth* and *his hand*) are being conceived as belonging to one and the same individual; this may be read as an attempt by the poet to disfigure the "he". Moreover, the comparison "his mouth" with "a dark cavern" where teeth are stalactites further intensifies the process of disfigurement of the male. This appears to be a step towards establishing (poetically) domination over the male. The method adopted is that of artful condemnation. The lexical items ''mouth'' and ''hand'' have the same semantic specification (+Human), while ''cavern'' is (-Human), (-Animate). This overt denial of individuality to the male partner is intended to serve as background to the assertion of the individuality of the speaker.

In line 6 the speaker uses a striking verb ''race'' to designate the building up of emotion and the resultant outburst of lust. However in the line that follows the force of the verb ''race'' is nullified by the lack-vigour expression ''wander''. Love thus becomes ''puddles of desire.'' In lines 8-9 the initial urgency of the act is lost. The physical description with which the poem began still goes on : in lines 9-10 the lover, though further distanced by the terms ''man'' (Cf. ''this man''), is still described as in action — with ''nimble fingertips'' he unleashes ''puddles of desire.'' Line 13 has another pronoun ''us''. This indicates that the man and the woman are alike atleast in sharing lust. The question in lines 12-14, which does not carry the necessary force, is indicative of the futility of the past and present. Still, it leaves a fragment of hope for the future.

The absence of a possessive pronoun in lines 14-15 marks laconic detachment : ''The heart'' appears where the form requires ''my heart''. Further the comparison of the heart with an artifact — ''cistern'', a mechanical construct — and the striking use of the verb ''fills'' (line 16) suggest total loss of feelings, The sexual encounters — both present and past — have resulted only in the mechanisation of the heart. The ellipsis after ''silence'' in line seventeen in significant because what is left unsaid is open for interpretation.

The appearance of the first person pronoun ''I'' in line 18 which is the subject of the assertive sentence ''I am a freak'' is important, for it strides over the ''he'' representing the male partner. The final declaration in the last three lines brings an end to the syntactic as well as semantic tension built up in the poem. The male partner has been left in his insubstantial state. The female emerges as a woman capable of making strong assertions;

here she asserts her individuality through the claim that she is a freak.

Kamala Das gives a free rein to her imagination in ‘‘The wild Bougainvillae’’ (SC). The persona’s disillusionment and the ongoing search for perfect freedom in a chaotic world of experiences seems to be her concern in it.

The Wild Bougainvillae

1. There was a time when I
2. Was sad in Calcutta, a few summer days
3. That passed slowly, and
4. Moodily, like mourners behind a bier. Days
5. When even my bed gave
6. No rest, but like a troubled sea, tossed me on
7. Its waves, and how I groaned
8. And moaned, and constantly yearned for a man from
9. Another town... Then, by
10. And by, my love wilted, for I took long walks,
11. Walked roads I had never
12. Seen before, saw faces I liked for their charm.
13. It is a good world, and
14. Packed with distractions. I walked through streets beside
15. The sea, where the barges
16. Float, their undersides rotting and the garbage
17. Rot, and the dead fish rot,
18. And, I smelt the smell of dying things and the
19. Heavy smell of rotting
20. Dead, I walked on streets where the night-girls with sham
21. Obtrusive breasts sauntered
22. And under yellow lamps, up-and-down wandered
23. Beaming their sickly smiles
24. At men. And, on streets near old cemeteries

Where the dead are so dead
That even their tombstones have lost their names in
The rains, and are pale now
And yellowed like grotesque teeth, a harvest of
Old teeth, and no mourner
Ever sheds a bouquet for them or tear
But, I did see beside
The older tombs some marigolds bloom and the
Wild red bougainvillae
Climbing their minarets. I walked, I saw and
I heard, the city tamed
Itself for me, and then my hunger for a
Particular touch waned
And one day I sent him some roses and slept
Through the night, a silent
Dreamless sleep and woke up in the morning free.

The theme of this poem is seen to revolve around two things : the speaker's inability to find a satisfactory source of love and her longing for freedom from emotional bondage. While the language of the poem exposes the emotional pressures within the speaker a distancing effect is achieved in the various images it creates. The world within the poem, for the most part, is temporal and chaotic while what is intended is liberation from bondage. The space-time continuum of the world within the poem reveals the poet's thoughts with that spontaneity which may receive the female reader's sympathetic attention. The thematic pattern that underlies a poem of this sort, which the language pattern mimes, is based on the play of emotions.

The language of this poem creates in the reader the cumulative impression that the personal emotions have been enfolded within a linguistic equivalent for a consistent world-view. The world created is a very real one the significance of which an ordinary perceiver may fail to realize. It is the repetitive/parallelistic lines that give the poem its langurous tone and rhythm.

The poem's most obvious stylistic feature is the repetition of the NP + VP structure :

I was sad in Calcutta (lines one-two)
I groaned (line seven)
I took long walks (line ten)
I had never seen... (lines eleven-twelve)
I liked (line twelve)
I walked (line fourteen)
I smelt (line eighteen)
I walked (line twenty)
I did see (line thirtyone)
I walked (line thirty four)
I heard (line thirty five)
I sent (line thirtyeight)

Syntactic parallelism of this sort, frequent in Kamala Das, gives the poem life (an almost similar syntactic repetition was noted in "An Introduction"). On the first reading itself the reader will know that the poem is a mimesis of the poet's experiences. These experiences are given manysided appearance through movement, shift in tone and emotion. It is the mimetic language of the poem that carries out all these functions.

The structural parallelism noted above points to the stylistic effect that is characteristic of the linguistic strategies Kamala Das adopts to enforce the underlying emotion. The first two lines imitate the opening of folk tales and fairy tales : "There was a time when I/was sad in Calcutta..." The tense signifies "timeless" past, the space, however, is definite. This is followed by references to a few days in that past, at that particular place. Those days, says Kamala Das's speaker, were slow and moody "like mourners behind a bier". This is suggestive of the mood of the speaker. The effect is further intensified by the feminine rhymes of lines 4 and 6.

The hazy atmosphere of the poem which the reader apprehends in the very first reading is created by the emphasis on modification and phrasal structures. These are sustained by modifications such as "slowly", "moodily", and "long". Structural repetition is initiated in the seventh line and internal rhyme ("groaned", "moaned", "yearned") gives the initial unifying effect. This is followed by a syntactic break in line nine effecting shift.

The speaker gives the listener (the reader) the impression that she is a 'sufferer' in the world of male 'crucifiers'. The shift from the 'inner' world of the speaker to the 'outer' world of reality (here she is one among the many, but carrying a uniqueness of her own) begins from line 9. Lines 9-40 picture the speaker as a wanderer experiencing the disgusting everyday realities — the rot, the corruption and the grotesque sights. It is the repetition of the "I" (subject)+ copula that syntactically unifies the rest of the poem. These clauses are sometimes inverted as verb — comp — subject (Cf. lines 11-12) thereby bringing forth the aesthetic appeal of the experience she narrates. In another words Kamala Das's formal devices achieve the poetic heightening discernible in these lines.

There is a harvest of sensory images in lines 15-19. The image of rottenness is effected through the foregrounded lexical items : "rotting ...rot..rot..rot...smelt...smell...smell.....rotting". The prominence of these lexical items creates the image of decomposition which has universal dimensions. This effect is strengthened by alliteration of/s/and/r/s/and/r/. In lines 20-24 Kamala Das brings in images of corruption. The compounding "night-girls", modifiers "sham", "obtrusive", "sickly" and verbs "sauntered", "wandered," all suggest disorderliness, destitution and the resultant corruption. Hence the turbulence of the inner world of the speaker is matched by the turbulence of the external world.

A close examination of the syntactic pattern of the poem will show the relation they have to the observations made here in. A few clues to the use of syntactic structures to mime the thoughts that underlie the poem have already been noted. The syntactic breaks and shifts on focus have been to superimpose human appeal on poetic appeal. In the beginning there is visible the poet's struggle with time, a force that dominates her poetic vision. But this attitude to time is ambivalent. This ambivalence becomes evident when she fails to find anything but decay and death in the world of reality at times, and at times when she visualises in the cycle of time not just death and decay but life and regeneration. The end of this poem shows, though vaguely, the emergence of the self not hampered by the dead and the decomposing. Hence, there is the ultimate celebration of joy in the attainment of mental freedom.

The stylistic significance of Kamala Das's sensitivity to time lies in the selection and arrangement of lexical items. "The Wild Bougainvillae" has a number of lexical items and images of time. "Summer", "day", "night", "old" "morning" are a few of them denoting time. The poem's predicate is the past tense and this is maintained throughout. Exceptions are the inclusion of past perfect in line eleven, present tense in line thirteen and the implied future of the last line. Further, the absence of modal auxiliaries is also significant. The tense system without the use of modals — suggesting mood — projects the poet's desire to detach herself from the webs of unhappiness. Thus, the grammatical pattern of the poem is the basis of its aesthetic appeal.

The tombstones (grinning like ghosts!) of the desolate grave yards where "...no mourner/Ever sheds a bouquet for them or tear" suggests desperation. However, the temporal adverb "ever" which may convey an unceasing state, used with the verb "shed" whose subject is "mourner" and whose objects are "bouquet" and "tear" impedes the effect of the image. That nature cares for those whom humans ignore seems to be the implied meaning of the image of the marigold bloom and climbing bougainvillae in that forsaken grave yard. The total immersion in time — in memory— and the implied projection of thoughts into the future seen in the last line shows that the speaker is locked in time which progresses and therefore not free from memories. Hence, future may not be much different from the past though the word "free" with which the poem ends signals a future life free from bonds.

The change made explicit in lines 34-37 and the consequent liberation from the "traps" of mind are temporal events. Since the time's progression depicted in the poem is arrow-like, changes are but natural. This means that the liberation indicated by "free" may be an indication of the beginning of further changes towards the ultimate realization of truth in the existence when the self encounters death. So the poet quite often transforms such haunting thoughts into poems. This, in other words, is a celebration of the tragic aspects of existence. In "The Dance of the Eunuchs" (SC) Kamala

Das telescopes the tragic aspects of life and constructs a vibrant world of emotions.

The Dance of the Eunuchs

1. It was hot, so hot, before the eunuchs came
2. To dance, wide skirts going round and round, cymbals
3. Richly clashing, and anklets jingling, jingling,
4. Jingling. Beneath the fiery gulmohur, with
5. Long braids flying, dark eyes flashing, they danced and
6. They danced, oh, they danced till they bled...There were green
7. Tattoos on their cheeks, jasmines in their hair, some
8. Were dark and some almost fair. Their voices
9. Were harsh, their songs melancholy; they sang of
10. Lovers dying and of children left unborn...
11. Some beat their drums; others their sorry breasts
12. And wailed, and writhed in vacant ecstacy. They
13. Were thin in limbs and dry, like half-burnt logs from
14. Funeral pyres, a drought and rottenness
15. Were in each of them. Even the crows were so
16. Silent on the trees, and the children, wide eyed, still;
17. All were watching these poor creatures' convulsions.
18. The sky crakled then, thunder came, and lightning
19. And rain, a meagre rain that smelt of dust in
20. Attics and the urine of lizards and mice...

It is well-known that in poetry the weight of meaning carried by an expression is substantially increased through artful repetition. In "The Dance of the Eunuchs" the emotional significance of the dance to the perceiving poet is iconically presented through lexical, syntactic and phonological repetition. The poem is the linguistic manifestation of a past experience. Needless to say the tense scheme suitable to the description of a past event is adopted.

The aesthetic appeal of the poem, however, rests on its syntax and imagery.

The repetition of the adjective "hot" with which the poem opens draws attention to the similarity between summer heat and heat in the dancing eunuchs. The adverbial repetition "round and round" and participial repetition "jingling," perceptually present the circular movement of the dancing eunuchs and create the visual image of the anklets and the auditory image of the sound the anklets make. In a similar vein the entire activity of the dance is perceptually presented through the clausal repetition "they danced and/They danced, oh, they danced till they bled..."

The disorder of things which the theme of the poem expounds is presented through inversion. Syntactic reiteration shows the exploitation of possible word orders to present the image of the swirling skirts, the flying braids, and the flashing eyes. Even things in nature are attune to the heat of their dance : the gulmohur too has a fiery look.

The physical movements of the eunuchs are presented through the manipulation of the syntax of the corresponding phrases. All through the poem syntactic rhythm, which is a characteristic of free verse reproduces the movement of these 'natural' dancers with remarkable accuracy. The repetition is little more than syntactic — it holds the background still while the eunuchs continue to "writhe" in "Vacant ecstacy". The repetitive/parallelistic structure appear thus :

Line 1. It was hot, so hot....

2. wide skirts going round and round

2-4. cymbals/Richly clashing, and anklets jingling, jingling/jingling....

5. Long braids flying, dark eyes flashing

5-6. they danced and /They danced, oh, they danced till they bled..

7. Tatoos on their cheeks, jasmines in their hair

7-8. Some/Were dark and some were almost fair

8-9. Their voices/Were harsh, their songs malancholy...

11. Some beat their drums; others beat their sorry breasts.

Beginning with the verbal repetition of the opening lines Kamala Das builds up the poem's aesthetic structure through the syntactic parrallelisms of these lines.

In the first six lines the poem's word-order seems to move in accordance with the eunuchs' macabre dance : the skirts swirl, the cybals sound, the anklets jingle, the braids fly and the eyes flash. In lines 6-8 the physical description of the eunuchs is given. Lines 8-10 give the theme of their song. The grotequeness of the dance is apparent in the beating of the breasts and the wailings of lines 11-12. (A powerful contradiction develops out of the drum beating and the breast beating, the songs and the wailings). In lines 13 and 14 the infertility and decay they represent is effected through comparisons. The stillness of everything except the eunuchs presented in lines 15-17 suggests again, along with other things, the grotesqueness and uncanniness of the dance.

The poem's imagery unfolds various aspects associated with the theme. The images, particularly similes and metaphors have special psychological significance. The writer's experience and environment are the twin factors that determine the nature and quality of his or her imagery. An author of Kamala Das's tradition and aesthetic sensibility only can think of such analogies at the sight of the dance of the sexually undifferentiated homosapiens. Her images appear thus :

> ....They
> Were thin in limbs and dry, like half-burnt logs from .....
> Funeral pyres, a drought and rottenness
> Were in each of them...
>
> ....
>
> The sky crackled then, thunder came, and lightning
> And rain, a meagre rain that smelt of dust in
> Attics and the urine of lizards and mice.

Stephen Ullmann holds that the existence of obsessive images is rooted in some highly personal traumatic experience. The recurrent images (for example, funeral pyre, burning, sea and sun in

Kamala Das) have often been interpreted by critics as symptoms of the writer's deeply rooted likes, dislikes and obsessions. As an example Ullmann points out the recurrence of insect imagery in Sartre's La *Nausée* : hands likened to a crab, tongue to a centipede; fingers moving like animals' legs. Such imagery with hallucinatory and surrealist quality are traced back to Sartre's childhood dislike for sea food.[34] Kamala Das's images in this poem — the macabre dance, the harsh and melancholic voices signing of death and decay, wailing and writhing, limbs like half-burnt logs in a funeral pyre, drought and rottenness and the rain that smells the urine of mice and lizards — all denote some traumatic experience which is haunting the speaker which might be traced back to her own disillusionment in life. The mirthlessness of sexual encounters and the fear of death and decay which Kamala Das repeatedly presents in her work form part of this traumatic experience. However, it should be noted that this is only one among the many aspects that create the uniqueness characteristic of her poetry.

Dissatisfaction in the sexual encounters validates the insubstantiality of men from the view point of the speaker. The sexual encounters lead to a more detailed analysis of the self in relation to men and to the masks the speaker wears as a corollary to her attempts. The awareness that life of this sort is mere pretence leads to the recognition that the self stands alone amid chaos. "Substitute" (DS), expounds this in detail.

Substitute

1. Memory
2. Great moody sea
3. Do not thump so
4. Against my shore.

5. Let me lie still
6. Without thought or will.
7. For a benign hour or two,
8. Dear night, be my tomb.

9. It is hard to believe
10. That I only lost,

Lost all, lost even
What I never had,

Life is quite simple now-
Love, blackmail and sorrow.

It will be all right when I learn
To paint my mouth like a clown's.
It will be all right if I put my hair,
Stand near my husband to make a proud pair.

It will be all right if I join clubs
And flirt a little over telephone.
It will be all right, it will be all right
I am the type that endures.

It will be all right, it will be all right
It will be all right between the world and me.
It will be all right if I don't remember
The last of the days together....

....Over market-square the poor crows
With raucous crics flailed the sky.
Our bodies after love-making
Turned away, rejecting.
Our words began to sound
Like clatter of swords in fight.

Yet, I was thinking, lying besides him
That I loved and was much loved.
It is physical thing, he said suddenly,
End it, I cried, end it, and let us be free;

This freedom was our last strange toy.
Like the hangman's robe, even while new
It could give no pride. Nor even joy.
We kissed and we loved, all in fury,
For another short hour or two
We went all warm and wild and lovely.

After that love became a swivel-door,
When one went out another came in.

Then I lost count, for always in my arms
Was a substitute for a substitute.
Oh, what is the use explaining —
It was a nameless faceless crowd.

All I remember is the first beautiful face
All I want to forget is that beautiful face.
It will be all right if I don't remember
That last of the days together.

It will be all right, it will be all right
It will be all right between the world and me.

The poem presents the theme of love and despair in vivid detail. Stylistic devices such as phrasal and clausal repetition, *anaphora*,[35] and *epanalepsis*[36] contribute to the rhythm of parallelism in this poem.

The word with which the poem begins and which is its first line is a temporal noun 'memory'. This has to do with the repetitive syntax of the poem, which shows repetition of phrases and clauses. A phrase is normally viewed as a sequence of words which function syntactically as a noun, adjective, or adverb and it has no finite verb. The clause includes both subject and predicate and the finite verb. If the finite verb elements are scarcely present, the resultant effect could be "stative" and this might push away the content of a given statement from the temporal state created by the tense system. In this vein a syntax dominated by phrases would, due the absence of finite verbs, tend to be stative. Because of this stativeness the content becomes conceptually stable. This is not so in a syntax dominated by clauses, because in such cases the content could be conceptually changing or temporal.[37] The interplay of temporal phrases and dynamic verbs has a significant function in Kamala Das's "Substitute."

In the first stanza the poet addresses the purely abstract, temporal 'memory' (thus personifying it), calls it "moody sea" and then forbids it from thumping against her "shore". The temporal noun "memory" followed by the dynamic verb "thump" sets the theme in motion. The lines too move showing variations in length. The speaker asks for leave from her own memory in order to enable her to be static — this is sponsored by the static verb "lie" and the static-noun "tomb" — while night is personified and asked to entomb her. This is what she does in the second stanza. Thus it is seen that the syntax of the first two stanzas is characterised by a mixture of stative phrases and dynamic clauses.

Another striking formal feature of Kamala Das's poetry is the co-ordinating structure. In this poem the 'pure' coordinator "and" occurs nine times and the co-ordinating conjunction "for" once. The personal pronoun "I" appears at fourteen places and "my" and "me" at there places. The finite verb elements governed by "I" in the third stanza are parallel. In the fifth stanza there is the clause "It will be all right" which is repeated in the succeeding three stanzas and in the last two. Since it is a clause which is repeated, this repetition suggests the dynamic nature of the events and experiences.

The definition of life in the fourth stanza as "love, blackmail and sorrow" suggests repetition of state as against the dynamism (change) of the preceding and succeeding stanzas. The clausal repetition while signalling the dynamic state of affairs is a case of semantic indirectness — the speaker by breaking the maxim of quality 'implicates' the 'unspoken' meaning. She is 'implicating' that the state of affairs is beyond normal, and thereby refers to the previously expressed idea that life is sorrow, lust and pretense. The static state of life suggested in the fourth stanza is contrasted in the mobility suggested in stanzas five-eight. All the lines in these stanzas except the last one in the eighth are clauses, suggesting dynamism and thus means that life is on the move. This contradicts the immobility implied in the fourth stanza.

In the ninth stanza change in rhythm is visible. The relapse to the temporal incident outside the personal life suggests the futility of the experience that she narrates : the poor crows/With raucous cries flailed the sky." In the tenth stanza (lines 29-30) terminal repetition of present participles ("love-making," "rejecting") deliver a sense of continual action. Line 32 is semantically parallel to line 31. This shows change in syntax, rhythm and tone. The coitus represented by the ineffective flailings of the crows — suggesting insufficiency and ephemerality — is validated in lines 29-32. The dynamic participials in this stanza add dimension to the mirthlessness of an act which ought to yield pleasure of a higher order. The loose syntactic structure of lines 27-32 therefore, mimes the detached feelings of the speaker.

It has been observed that the repetitive structures generate the poem's aesthetic appeal. But how the repetitive/parallelistic structures develop structurally poses a problem. Barbara H. Smith's comment seems to be worthwhile in this context : "Where repetition is the fundamental principle of thematic generation, the resulting structure will tend to be *paratactic*, that is, the coherence of the poem will not be dependent on the sequential arrangement of its major thematic units."[38] Lines 1 to 12 (the first three stanzas), 15 to 18 (fifth stanza), 25 to 32 (stanzas eight and nine) 43-44 (twelfth stanza) and 49-52 (fourteenth stanza) have paratactic structure. Lines 33 to 36 have *anaphora* and *epanalepsis* as repetitive devices denoting the transcient nature of the affair with the lover and the consequential repulsion. In the tenth stanza (lines 33 to 36) the linking of the finite verb with the first person subject "I" gives prominence to the speaker's indulgence and desire to liberate herself from the emotional servitude. *Anaphora* is again the repetitive device in lines 37-42 (eleventh stanza) where Kamala Das uses simple past as against the present progressive and simple present of the preceding stanza. Here the speaker's presence is not direct since the affair itself is predominant. Therefore, in the subject position we find the plural pronoun "we". Though the narration in this stanza is in simple past, its structure suggests a sense of timelessness. This sense of timelessness is indicative of the speaker's feeling of detachment even while physically attached to her sexual partner.

"It will be all right," is the chief repetend in the poem. This occurs twelve times. In between and before its occurrence Kamala Das employs *anaphora* to provide a syntactic and semantic context for the poem. For instance *anaphora* is used effectively in lines 11, 34 and 39. It's first use is noticed when the persona speaks about her sense of loss — or real pleasure — in the sexual encounters and the next when she expresses what was in her fancy about love. The third use is when she refers back to the previously expressed notion of freedom.

Lines 37-39 present an apt comparison picturing a traumatic

experience. The comparison of freedom with a hangman's new robe suggests hopelessness of a higher order. Sexual unions are but violent physical indulgence. The total loss of real pleasure and the consequent moral collapse is projected in lines 45-48. Her lovers thus become a nameless, faceless crowd and she a whore.

In the syntactically parallel lines 49-50 the poet returns to the temporal realm of memory and reintroduces the repented "It will be all right" to complete the rhythmic frame work. In the closing lines the visible inclination towards a passive role in love making receives emphasis from the term "forget". The repetition of the clause "It will be all right" while implicating the repeated happening of the undesirable establishes that fulfilment and reality are poles apart. Thus, the speaker affirms that she is an estranged being; the only link between her and the world is the mask of pretence. The estranged writer's love for oblivion is recreated in "Luminol" (DS)

Luminol

1. Love-lorn,
2. It is only
3. Wise at times to let sleep
4. Make holes in memory, even
5. If it
6. Be the cold and
7. Luminous sleep banked in
8. The heart of pills, for he shall not
9. Enter
10. Your ruthless one,
11. Being human, clumsy
12. With noise and movement, the soul's mute
13. Arena,
14. That silent sleep inside your sleep.

This is yet another of those short poems of Kamala Das depicting an intensely personal situation. The poem has only fifty five words. However, the syntactic and semantic features make it one of her best pieces.

The meaning of the compound word "love-lorn" which constitutes the first line of the poem carries the clue to the theme of the poem : it is about the love for oblivion, to escape into the world of forgetfulness, when true love is absent. The subject matter will be clear when the structure is looked at from near.

In normal syntax there should be an animate agent to instigate the action the verb describes.[39] In this poem there are verbs with and without agents.

Without agent	**With agent**
It is only wise	Sleep make holes ("Sleep" is the inanimate agent of the verb "make". It is not an animate instigator, hence doesnot follow rules of grammar. The use of "sleep" as an agent is thus figurative).
The cold and luminous sleep banked in the heart of pills	
He shall not enter	

Assymetry is seen in the above categorisation. All the finite verbs except "make" have subjects which cannot be identified as agents (instigator of the action described by the verb). "Sleep" is the agent of the verb "make". However, the verb "make" requires an animate agent which "sleep" is not. Hence, personification of "sleep" is necessary for the sentence to be meaningful. It is curious to note that there is no non-finite verb in the poem. The assymetry discernible is the outcome of the absence of an animate agent where there should be one, while an inanimate agent is supplied in the single case where the finite verb has an agent. So these finite verbs are further divided into verbs which can never take an agent and those which can :

Which cannot take agent : is, banked, enter, shall; which can take agent : make

"Is" does not describe an action and so its subject is not an agent. "Shall" expresses mood and so does not take an agent. The verb "banked" describes an action that has happened to the subject. But the subject cannot bring about this action through its own instigation. Similar is the case of "let" which itself is not an action. However, the finite verb ''make'' can take an agent, which in this case is the abstraction ''sleep''. This offers contrast to the rest of the finite verbs that cannot take an agent. Thus, the assymetry in the poem is due to the occurrence of finite verbs with grammatical subjects which are not agents, the only exception being the existence of an agent which, semantically, cannot function as an agent.

The fact that all except one of the finite verbs in the poem are without agents has important implications. If the absence of any true agentive phrase is accepted as part of the poet's aesthetics, it might mean that the lines after the coordinating conjunction ''for'' (line eight-twelve) would not mean the following :

> He shall not enter
> Who is your ruthless one
> Who is human
> Who is clumsy with movement

The above hypothetical construct is semantically identical to the corresponding lines in the poem except for the deletion of the surface agents. This much linguistic detail might help think about the relationship between the syntax of the poem and its meaning. Why is there an absence of the agents of action? The forlorn state is a state initiated not by any agent or agents as such. It is the product of circumstances. Therefore, in the world within the poem there is no initiator of action. It might seem for a while that the ''he'' of the eighth line is the agent. But in a world where drug induced sleep blocks the hallucinations of the lover, an agent is absolutely unnecessary.

Another stylistic aspect helping to comprehend the poem's meaning is its tense system. All the verbs except ''banked'' which is there to serve a special purpose, are in simple present. This shows that the poet does not intend to say anything about any action in progress. To describe an action progressing through time there should be the present progressive tense. The absence of a true agent confirms this aspect. The ''ing'' form in ''being'' though resembles present progressive, actually draws attention to the absence of the progressive aspect. Hence, the simple present tense of lines 8-9 (''he shall not/Enter'') introduces transitoriness. This receives emphasis from lines 10-13 where transitoriness is implied. Here is thus focus on person and action that happen in time. However, the present tense in lines 2-4 ("it is only/ Wise at times, to let sleep/Make holes in memory...") seems to express a universal truth which is outside of time. This contrasts with the transitoriness mentioned above.

The syntactic and semantic features are consistent with the poem's theme. The poem expounds a state which is not the creation of any particular individual. Intuitively it is understood that this state is the product circumstances. The timelessness imparted to the actions through the choice of simple present tense creates the poem's world : a world of forgetfulness, which is without agency and hence absolute. It is like death which is timeless and absolute. In "Herons" *(Collected Poems 1)* she presents an almost similar theme in an equally effective language.

Herons

1. On sedatives
2. I am more lovable
3. Says my husband
4. My speech becomes a mistladen terrain
5. The words emerge tinctured with sleep
6. They rise the still coves of dreams
7. In unhurried flight like herons...
8. And my ragdoll limbs adjust better
9. To his versatile lust....he would if he could
10. Sing lullabies to his wife's sleeping soul
11. Sweet lullabies to thicken its swoon
12. On sedatives
13. I grow more lovable
14. Says my husband.

Two important stylistic devices used in this poem which explain the poet's thematic strategy are parallelism and ellipsis. Their employment is important in this poem because it is the patterned repetition and parallelism that give the poem its "closed" structure. The last three lines are a repetition of the first three and in between them there are the syntactically parallel lines with ellipsis in the seventh .and ninth.

Parallelism, as already noted, shows the poet's aesthetic response to emotions. In "Herons" Kamala Das handles the syntactic patterns with skill to give the poem a 'closed' structure. The patterned repetition is to create a sense of loss. It evokes the feeling that the personal emotions are enveloped in the structural framework of the poem. This gives the reader a 'vision' of an 'illegitimate' sex experience with a legitimate partner.

The parallelistic and repetitive pattern of the poem does not show diffusion of feelings. Everything related to the speaker around whom the theme is built is stagnant. The language of the poem imitates the drowsy passive state of the woman's body under the impact of sedatives. It gives the feeling that the speaker's husband is a pervert whose lust is unleashed when she is in a semiconscious state.

In line 4 the finite verb "become" which cannot take an agent, which describes a state, but which is not itself an action reinforces the vagueness suggested by its object "a mist laden terrain". Here the effect created is that of a speech coming out of a person who is in a semiconscious state. The images that appear in succession in the following lines give the poem its "dazed" sensuousness :

> My speech becomes a mistladen terrain
> The words emerge tinctured with sleep
> They rise from the still coves of dreams
> In unhurried flight like herons...

The syntactic break or ellipsis in lines 7 and 9 suggests fading tone, as if the drug is taking control over the entire body. Ellipsis is important as a stylistic tool because it can act as a cohesive device. (In transformational grammar it is called deletion). The sound pattern produced by syntax suggests languor; the speaker's voice seems to fade at the point where syntax breaks in ellipsis.

The collocation of "sleep", "dreams" and "swoon" shows textual cohesion because they are related to the same idea. The reiteration in lines 12-14 achieves an interesting effect : the state described in the middle of the poem is the inner state, while the three lines in the beginning and end provide the outer cover. Thus, the speaker is enveloped by two active forces, one chemical, and the other human, that is, the sedatives and her husband.

Sex obsession and the accompanying imagery of death have existential as well as metaphorical values in Kamala Das's poems. In traditional Indian poetry treating Krishna Myth, sexual union of Radha and Krishna is metaphorical; it signifies the union of "prakrti" and "purusha". But the same assumes different magnitude in Kamala Das. In Kamala Das's hands too Krishna and Radha are lovers, but she does not grab them with the vestments of "Bhakti". Her concern is not religious, it is existential and literary. Kamala Das, like Vidyapati who exemplifies the sexual relationship of Radha and Krishna, throws a literary focus through which she tries to express the intensity of human sexual relationship.[40] Such of her poems may also be expressive of the "almost paranoid concern" she expresses towards death.[41] Two of her poems treating Krishna myth — "Radha" (DS) and "Ghanashyam" (CPI)- are examined.

Radha

1. The long waiting
2. Had made their bond so chaste, and all the doubting

3. And the reasoning
4. So that in his first true embrace, she was girl

5. And virgin crying
6. Everything in me
7. Is melting, even the hardness at the core
8. O Krishna, I am melting, melting, melting

9. Nothing remains but
10. You....

This short poem with only fifty one words is another example of Kamala Das's mastery over language. The feeling the lines convey is intense; the imagery is powerful.

The mythological associations of the proper noun "Radha" illustrates how a word may create an aesthetic effect. The power of such words to give rise to pleasant or unpleasant overtones is summarised in the following passage in Boileau's *Art Poetique* :

> Mythology offers a thousand different pleasures to the mind. There are all the happy names seem born for the verse, Ulysses, Agamemnon, Orestes...Sometimes the hard or bizarre sound of a single name renders a whole poem ludicrous or barbarous.[42]

The title of the poem thus offers aesthetic delight, to the reader who knows Krishna Myth. The motif (the mythical names), is to assert the poet's individuality while giving along with it a pleasurable sensuous experience. How the structure of the poem presents the experience and how the syntax suggests fusion of the self and the imaginary source of pleasure is to be seen. This necessitates a consideration of the iconic potential of the poem's syntax. Richard D. Cureton makes the following observation about iconic syntax :

> ...poets often exploit the iconic potential of linguistic signs : the ability of these signs to both to refer to a concept or express a proposition and, at the same time, "present" a perceptual experience to which that concept or proposition applies. While what these iconic features add to a literary work is purely experiential and, consequently, adds life to the conceptual content of the work, these structures contribute to two important dimension of the work's aesthetic structure. Firstly, since iconic features "present" (as well as refer), they add perceptual immediacy to the work. In some sense, they build the "world" conveyed by the conceptual content of the work directly into the medium for its communication. Second, because their "presentational" aspect is technically "meaningless", these structures provide the ultimate way of "saying" something indirectly, thus, granting additional subtlety to the writers's expressive means.[43]

The syntactic icon noticeable in "Radha" is fusion — the fused sentences bear the conceptual content "union". In "Radha" Kamala Das uses fused structures in order to present thematic fusion. The poem's main syntactic break is the ellipsis in the end. In between the beginning and the end there are only six commas introducing brief pauses and leaves out full-stops that would make long syntactic break. This absence of full-stops shortens the break between clauses and makes possible a close knit reading of the structure. The asyndetic structure of the poem further helps the fusion of the theme. The grammatical subject of the sentence with which the poem is constituted is the noun phrase "The long waiting". The adjective "chaste" works to give clausal structure to the otherwise incomplete syntax of "and all the doubting/And reasoning." The adverb clause of manner initiated by "so that" in line 4 carries over the impact of the subject noun phrase and that of the verb "embrace" till the end where the second person pronoun "you" visually presents the fusion.

The preceding discussion helps form opinion about the relation between the syntactic units and what they exemplify. Nine distinct constructions could be made out of the poem :

> The long waiting had made their bond so chaste
> The long waiting had made all the doubting so chaste
> The long waiting had made all the reasoning so chaste
> [So that] In his first true embrace she was virgin crying
> [And] Everything in me is melting
> [And] Even the hardness at the core is melting
> [And] O Krishna, I am melting, I am melting, I am melting
> [And] O Krishna, nothing remains but you

These constructions express the conceptual content of the poem. The interaction between myth and reality is implied in the fusion of the lover and the beloved. The lexical repetition in the eighth line imitates the process of melting so that the reader is imparted the experience in all its intensity. The woven syntactic structure of the poem exemplified above perceptually present the fusion of myth and reality-of the metaphorical union of Radha and Krishna and the poet's yearning for a blissful union with the absent.

The union of the love pair, which is the conceptual content of the poem is thus presented in unusually condensed language. The reader, while understanding the metaphor, also experiences the fusion initiated by the syntax. In lines 1-5 the long waiting and this coming together is presented. Lines 5-10 depict Radha's "melting" and her fusion with her lover. Thus, Kamala Das's treatment offers contrast to the *ardhanareeswara* concept where woman is fused to man but yet remains distinguishable. Oneness, which is the outcome is syntactically represented by the pronoun "you" which is the last line of the poem.

There is a marked difference between those of Kamala Das's poems that celebrate self and sensuality with the help of myth and those without. In her love poems that involve Krishna myth, linguistic sign depicts the present while its metaphorical value depicts the absent. Hence, the present "sign" implies an absent abstraction. In the erotic poems discussed earlier lesser presence of abstraction was noticed. In love poems there is an abundance of this because the presence of pure love is a rare event to be expressed in concrete terms. In "Ghanashyam" (CPI) the metaphorically present Krishna is the lover whom the speaker expects to put an end to her longings. As has been mentioned earlier, her main concern seems to be literary and existential though a union deeper than the physical is suggested.

Ghanashyam

1. Ghanashyam,
2. You have like a koel built your nest in the arbour of my heart.
3. My life, until now a sleeping jungle is at last astir with music
4. You led me along a route I have never known before
5. But at each turn when I near you
6. Like a spectral flame you vanish
7. The flame of my prayer lamp holds captive my future
8. I gaze into the red eye of death
9. The hot stare of truth unveiled.
10. Life is moisture
11. Life is water, semen and blood
12. Death is drought
13. Death is the hot sauna leading to cool rest-rooms
14. Death is the last, lost sob of the relative
15. Beside the red walled morgue.
16. O Shyam, my Ghanashyam
17. With words I weave a raiment for you
18. With songs a sky

19. With such music I liberate in the oceans their fervid dances
20. We played once a husk-game, my lover and I
21. His body needing mine,
22. His ageing body in its pride meeting the need for mine
23. And each time his lust was quietened
24. And he turned his back on me
25. In panic I asked don't you want me any longer, don't you want me
26. Don't you, don't you?
27. In love when the snow slowly began to fall
28. Like a bird I migrated to warmer climes
29. That was my only method of survival
30. In this tragic game the unwise, like children, play
31. And often lose in.
32. At three in the morning
33. I wake trembling from dreams of a stark white loneliness
34. Like bleached bones cracking in the desert sun was my loneliness,
35. And each time my husband,
36. His mouth bitter with sleep,
37. Kisses, mumbling to me of love,
38. But if he is you and I am you
39. Who is loving who
40. Who is the husk who the kernel
41. Where is the body where is the soul
42. You come in strange forms
43. And your names are many.
44. Is it then a fact that I love the disguise
45. And the name more than I love you?
46. Can I consciously weaken bonds?
47. The child's umbilical cord shrivels and falls

48. But new connections begin, new traps arise
49. And new pains
50. Ghanashyam
51. The cell of the eternal sun,
52. Then blood of the eternal fire,
53. The hue of the summer air
54. I want a peace that I can tote
55. Like an infant in my arms
56. I want a peace that will doze
57. In the whites of my eyes when I smile
58. The ones in saffron robes told me of you
59. And when they left
60. I thought only of what they left unsaid
61. Wisdom must come in silence
62. When the guests have gone
63. The plates are washed
64. And the lights put out
65. Wisdom must steel in like a breeze
66. From beneath the shuttered door
67. Shyam O Ghanashyam
68. You have like a fisherman cast your net in the narrows
69. O my mind
70. And towards you my thoughts today
71. Must race like enchanted fish...

The poem begins with an address to the invisible lover Ghanashyam (the cloud coloured, Krishna). Ghanashyam, the flute player, is compared to the beautifully singing black bird koel. The simile further explains the relation between the speaker and the invisible lover — the bird (Ghanashyam) building a nest in the arbour (her heart). This is followed by an apt metaphor in the third line, "My life until now a sleeping jungle is at last astir with music." "Now" indicates time, but it is metaphorical and has nothing to do with the immediate present of the speaker's life.

The comparison of the speaker's life with a sleeping jungle and the entering of Krishna, like the koel arriving at the forest, making it astir with music have powerful effects. The myth giving her incitement to poetic creativity is thus beautifully suggested in the first three lines. The 5th line which tells about the vanishing of Krishna like a "spectral flame" gives exphasis of this contrast. The syntactic juxtaposition of the two images suggests the illusory presence of the lover and brings in the awareness that he is absent.

The twin metaphors "the red eye of death" and "the hot stare of truth" mark a sudden shift : they break the illusion and expose the self to its "own most possibility," death.[44] The metaphorical explanation of the speaker's view is then given in the following images where the abstractions "life" and "death" are given concrete parallels :

Life is moisture

-C +C

Life is water, semen and blood

-C +C

Death is drought

-C +C

Death is the hot sauna leading to cool rest-roms

-C +C

These syntactically parallel lines are metaphoric substitutes of the speaker's cognition of the self and the reality that awaits for an encounter. It appears that Kamala Das, by the syntax representing the abstract entities and their concrete parallels is presenting a progression towards nothingness. This nothingness represented by the metaphors of death is a representation individuality, because the death of an individual cannot be imitated by another. Thus, the mythical experience gradually gives way to existential truth. However the last lines of the poem offer this a contrast.

In the midst of visionary awarenesses appear the concrete experience, namely the sexual encounters with the speaker's lover. In coordinate syntax (lines 20-26) she presents the experience she shared with her lover. The co-ordinate syntax co-ordinates the superficial event of love making and the sense of abandonment. This distressing account of reality serves the purpose of creating 'angst', which takes her to the mythical lover. This description of real encounters interrupts the empathic escape into tho roalm of myth. The repeated questions of lines 25-26 signals the future non-possibility of real pleasure giving experiences.

What prepared the background for the empathic escape is the disillusionment presented in suggestive imagery : "In love when the snow slowly began to fall/Like a bird I migrated to warmer climes." The preposing of the adverbial clause creates an impact which aptly conveys the shift in the speaker's life. The loneliness implied in these lines receive additional intensity in lines 33-34 "....a stark white loneliness,/Like bleached bones cracking in the desert sun was my loneliness." The poetiser NRM *Stark white* which is followed by the simile of bleaching bones present a visual image suggesting terrible heat and dehydration and signify the horror experienced when one feels abandoned.

The self's yearning for communion with the absent is taken up again in the following lines :

> But if he is you and I am you
> Who is loving who
> Who is the husk and who the kernel
> Where is the body where is the soul

The syntax imitates, as has been observed in the discussion of "Radha", the hypothetical coercion of the absent and the present. In the imagery of these lines the sensuousness and immediacy of the previous lines is seen receding into the vague, illusory absence of abstraction. In lines 46-49 this is replaced by existential experience. "The childs umbilical cord," a quite unexpected element, takes the perceiving reader to the prenatal condition, and to the first feeling of abandonment on birth.

The merging of the 'present' and 'absent' realities is a complex state where exist vision, sensuality and disillusionment. The despair of the present is lost in the metaphors picturing Ghanasyam : "The cell of the eternal sun, /the blood of the eternal fire, /The hue of the summer air.... "The fading of this vision of Ghanashyam into the images of 'present' reality picturing the fate of a woman marks the shift which is a characteristic feature of this poem.

The last five lines of the poem depict happiness in the captivity of illusion. Here Ghanashyam is 'presence' as well as 'absence'. His net too is both 'presence' and 'absence'. The persona's mind is an enchanted fish that races into the captor's net. The absent Ghanashyam is, therefore, an abstraction that provides her happiness. This indicates the speaker's escape into the realm of the absent through the empathic energies of poetry.

In sum, Kamala Das's presentation of experience in "Ghanashyam" depends upon imagery and syntax that suggest metaphoric progression in a dialectic between presence and absence. The harmony seen in the presentation of poetic vision and everyday reality is due to her sense of creativity. The ideal of the invisible absent evoked through artificial vision alternatively gives way to physical presence of everyday realities. The mythic and the mundane are in tension as well as in harmony between what is imagined to be and what actually is.

While her purpose is the celebration of self and sensuality, Kamala Das never forgets to depict the different moods of the existential searcher. In order to achieve this she may resort to myth or reality or both. In "The Old Playhouse" (*The Old Playhouse and other Poems*) she makes full use of her poetic idiom to construct a perceptually stable framework for her thoughts.

The Old Playhouse

1. You planned to tame a swallow, to hold her
2. In the long summer of your love so that she would forget
3. Not the raw seasons alone, and the homes left behind, but
4. Also her nature, the urge to fly, and the endless
5. Pathways of the sky. It was not to gather knowledge
6. Of yet another man that I came to you but to learn
7. What I was, and by learning, to learn to grow, but every

8. Lesson you gave was about yourself. You were pleased
9. With my body's response, its weather, its usual shallow
10. Convulsions. You dribbled spittle into my mouth, you poured
11. Yourself into every nook and cranny, you enbalmed
12. My poor lust with your bitter-sweet juices. You called me wife,
13. I was taught to break saccharine into your tea and
14. To offer at the right moment the vitamins. Cowering
15. Beneath your monstrous ego I ate the magic loaf and
16. Became a dwarf. I lost my will and reason, to all your
17. Questions I mumbled incoherent replies. The summer
18. Begins to pall. I remember the ruder breezes
19. Of the fall and the smoke from the burning leaves. Your room is
20. Always lit by artificial lights, your windows always
21. Shut, Even the air-conditioner helps so little,
22. All pervasive is the male scent of your breath. The cut flowers
23. In the vases have begun to smell of human sweat. There is
24. No more singing, no more dance, my mind is an old
25. Playhouse with all its lights put out. The strong man's technique is
26. Always the same, he serves his love in lethal doses,
27. For, love is Narcissus at the water's edge, haunted
28. By its own lonely face, and yet it must seek at last
29. To shatter and the kind night to erase the water.

This poem, for the most part, is an address by the present "I" to the absent "you". In most of the poems of Kamala Das with an "I" and a "you" the context in some way is a mimesis of dramatic dialogue — an "I" addressing a "you" who is supposed to be the husband or lover. In this case the speaker explicitly states that it is her husband (Cf. line 12, "you called me wife").

In the first line of the poem the speaker pictures herself as the untamable migratory bird "Swallow", while her addressee is only "you". The tense system of the poem is this : past tense in lines 1-17, present tense in lines 25-28 and future time (implied) in the last three lines. However, as an isolated fact this is of no significance. What is of interest is how the choices pattern together.

The second person pronoun "you" which is placed in the thematic position appears thirteen times, and "I" and "me" appear ten times. The third person "she",/"her" occur only three times. The personal noun "man" occurs twice and "wife" once. These pronouns and personal nouns occur with both present and past tenses, thereby bridging the past with the present. This is seen to happen in conformity with the semantic tension between immediacy and non-immediacy of temporal and spatial reference. However, the future time does not mark any human presence — it occurs with an abstraction referring to total freedom. This accounts for the grammatical cohesion in the poem.

Lexical cohesion is a striking stylistic feature of this poem. This is achieved through the repetition of "love" (three times), "summer" (twice) and "learn" (three times). Apart from this, the selection of words is mostly confined to those which maintain a semantic connection with other items in the poem. Thus, semantic connection runs through "night", "season", "weather" and "fall"; "swallow" and "dwarf", "nature", "urge", "lust", "ego", and "freedom"; "home", "room", "window", and "play-house"; "knowledge" and "lesson"; "dribble", "pour" and "enbalm"; "saccharine", "tea", "vitamins", and "loaf"; "monstrous", "magic" "lethal" and "haunt". This list sufficiently illustrates the way the poem's meaning is patterned — the relationships are tightly organised. This covers the selectional (paradigmatic) aspects that direct the reader towards the 'life centre' of the poem.

In metaphors exist semantic oddity, a linguistic form demanding non-normal interpretation. In "the long summer of your love" (line two) there is clash between "summer" and "love"; however, if we substitute "summer" with "ecstacy" which does not refer to time but to human, the line loses its aesthetic appeal. This helps group the important stylistic features in the poem : (i) those that suggest psychological states and (ii) those that consist in the use of lexical items creating wild images. Those that denote psychological states are "learn to grow", "you poured yourself", "embalmed my poor lust", "monstrous ego", "male scent of your breath", "my mind is an old/Playhouse", "love in lethal doses", and "love is Narcissus at water's edge". Those that create wild images are "raw seasons", "magic loaf", "the summer/Begins to pall" and "ruder breezes". These features explain the mental state of the individual whose right to live free has been infringed upon by other people.

Earlier certain pattern of similarities was noted in the poem's deviant lexical items. The cohesion of schemes too is apparent. The syntactic parallelism of the order noun phrase + verb phrase (NP + VP) with which the poem begins is repeated especially in : "You dribbled spittle into my mouth, you poured/Yourself into every nook and cranny, you enbalmed/My poor lust with your bitter sweet juices. You called me wife,..." It is seen that formal parallelism of this sort coincides with the rhythmic units.

The formal features consulted in the preceding paragraphs are part of the meaning of the poem, and they, among other things, serve as factors helping interpretation. Since the foregrounded elements cited are metaphorical expressions, they require information outside linguistic description. Thus, the lexical items and the parallelism noted above point towards a conflict between the addresser and the addressee. They also point towards the cause for the grievances of the speaker (addresser) and her predictions about future.

The "I" and "you" in the poem and the circumstances in which the speaker is communicating the poem's message can be taken up once again for scrutiny. From the larger context the "I" is identified as the poet herself, and from the poem's context the "you" is identified as her husband. Taking this as the starting point we can follow the implications of the situation in which the poet addresses an absent individual who happens to be her husband.

The excessive use of the first person pronoun "I" and the positive qualities attributed to it through lexical associations and those features that are associated to the "you" suggest that the poem is about the psychological state of the speaker. The association of the "I" with lexical items "swallow" and "dwarf", "love" and "lust", "dribble", "pour", "enbalm," "tea", "vitamine", "ego", and "room" have the following implications. "Swallow" implies freedom — it is a swift flying bird which migrates to warmer countries. Thus, along with freedom the term implies sexual licence too, which is voiced in many of Kamala Das's poems. However, contrary to this, restrictions have been imposed upon her — thus the relevance of the term "dwarf". The term "love", at many places in Kamala Das's poetry, is synonymous to "lust" and hence the love suggested has its roots in the body. This desire of the body, as her attitude suggests, cannot be fulfilled under the restraints of the confinement in a splendid house. The association of "love" with "knowledge" implies the interpretation that it is through "love" which means sexual-intercourse that she wants to know herself and establish her identity. Contrary to this what was in her lot was psychological reduction ("dwarf"), under the 'temporal power', husband. Sex experience with the husband is exemplified through the suggestion of disgust and ephemerality : dribbling spittle into mouth, pouring and enbalming with bitter sweet juices. The boredome of life under the husband's control is suggested through the description of routine activities such as breaking of saccharine into tea, giving vitamins, and the reference to the room of confinement. The parallelism in lines 10-12 builds implications of similarity between the "you" (husband) and the boredom of sex with him.

In sum the aim of the poet seems to be to establish that her speaker wants to uphold her individuality which her husband perpetually attempts to destroy. He belittles her by confining her in himself through loathsome sex-acts and household work. The woman, however, is determined to establish her individuality through liberating herself from the 'marriage-herse'. This is presented through the suggestive imagery of the last lines :

> For, love is Narcissus at the water's edge, haunted
> By its own lonely face, and yet it must seek at last
> An end, a pure, total freedom, it must will the mirrors
> To shatter and the kind night to erase the water.

The search for identity unveiled in the above discussion is an important aspect of Kamala Das's work. The presence of the husband seems to be primarily the cause for the absence of a name and identity which partly forms the aim of the speaker's search. Like Kahlil Gibran's prophet she seems to propogate that marriage cannot be a bondage because one cannot keep another's heart in confinement. The truth, as Gibran might argue, is that only the hand of life can contain the hearts. In ''The Stone Age'' (OP) Kamala Das treats the same theme adding extra dimensions to it.

The Stone Age

1. Fond husband, ancient settler in the mind,
2. Old fat spider, weaving webs of bewilderment,
3. Be kind. You turn me into a bird of stone, a granite
4. Dove, you build round me a shabby drawing room,
5. And stroke my pitted face absent-mindedly while
6. You read. With loud talk you bruise my pre-morning sleep,
7. You stick a finger into my dreaming eye. And
8. Yet on day dreams strong men cast their shadows, they sink
9. Like white suns in the swell of my Dravidian blood,
10. Secretly flow the drains beneath sacred cities.
11. When you leave, I drive my blue battered car
12. Along the bluer sea. I run up the forty
13. Noisy steps to knock at another's door.
14. Through peepholes, the neighbours watch,
15. They watch me come
16. And go like rain. Ask me, everybody, ask me
17. What he sees in me, ask me why he is called a lion,
18. A libertine, ask me the flavour of his
19. Mouth, ask me why his hand sways like a hooded snake

20. Before it clasp my pubis. Ask me why like
21. A great tree, felled, he slumps against my breasts,
22. And sleeps. Ask me why life is short and love is
23. Shorter still, ask me what is bliss and what its price...

Thematically, the poem is in part an extension of "The Old Playhouse". But the formal features that purport the poet's thoughts are different. Elsewhere it is observed that artistic merit lies in the way the writer presents his/her impressions and experiences. The way Kamala Das presents her existentialist speaker's experiences in this poem has the merit of being a presentational novelty within the sphere not only of her poetry but also of the Indian English poetry in general.

The formal patterns of the poem are capable of drawing the reader's attention to the lexical paradigms. This, in turn, paves way to the interpretation of the relationship between these paradigms. In the first three lines, that is, in "Fond husband, ancient settler in the mind/Old fat spider, weaving webs of bewilderment, Be kind..." linguistic clues to interpretation are apparent. At the phonological level the internal rhyme of words in the first line and alliteration of /f, /w/, and /b/ and at the syntactic level the equivalence between "Fond husband" and "Old fat spider" give preliminary clue to the interpretation. While poetic conventions might hold that the relationship between "husband" and "spider" evolves a metaphor, the syntagmatic parallel between the words prompts us to look for paradigmatic relations between them. In order words in the poem's context we may have to regard them equivalent in meaning. The picture we get out of this relationship is that of a merciless being and its defenceless victim.

The foregrounded paradigm denoting physical and mental torture has an important role in the first seven lines. "Webs", "bird of stone", "granite dove", "stroke", "bruise", and "stick" create the desired impact. The prominence of the verbs denoting torture and nouns denoting the hardness of the situation give a clear picture of the mental state of the victim. The word "stick" used as a verb accumulates overtones of pain and suffering. The torture which is distinctively projected in these lines further develop into further actions.

The lines about the pain inflicted upon the speaker by her husband and its aftermath, that is, the search for an illicit partner, make clear the sense carried by the syntax. The suppression of the speaker's individuality by her husband becomes an incentive to celebrate the pleasure of being an individual. Syntactic and phonological parallelisms encourage this interpretation. Lines 1, 2, 3, 4, 7, and 11, 12 have syntactically parallel constructions. The repetition of "Ask me...." (seven times) while contributing to the rhythm, condenses discourse and simplifies style. The metaphor of the "spider" is powerful. This contradiction — the viewing of the husband who should be the source of comfort and companionship as the destroyer of all these — is in effect an outright criticism of the institution of marriage. Similarly the apparent statement about "bliss" marks the growth of the idea given in the opening lines.

The twin images "bird of stone" and "granite dove" which appear in lines 3-4, while contributing to the rhythm, have other implications as well. A bird of stone is a bird carved out of stone for show. This suggests the sad state of the speaker. The term "granite dove" implies further meaning. A dove is a pretty innocent bird which cannot withstand any attack. A stone image of it symbolizes the frozen state of beauty and innocence. This offers contradiction to the idea contained in the image of the spider and his web. In the conflicting presence of these images lie the message of the poem.

Units of meaning such as "his hand... before it claps my pubis", and "he slumps against my breasts", which may find parallels in 'avant-garde' pornography, show the search for pleasure at its prime. However the "ask me" sequence in which the above units are embeded gives them extra meaning.

In short, the "I" and "you" relationship is explained in the first eleven lines through appropriate syntactic structures. The images in these lines show the husband as a loveless and cruel man — loveless in not giving the speaker a blissful experience and cruel in keeping her in confinement. The visual point of view is within the house, more particularly in the drawing room with the husband as the dictator of that world. In lines 11-16 the reader sees the speaker outside this world. This is only for a short while and soon she is in another world, in the company of another man.

From line 16 on a series of phrases occur depicting the woman's affair with the man designated as "he" and her existential approach to love and life. The "ask me" series end with this approach culminating in the expression of the expense at which bliss could be obtained. The same thought persists in "Glass" (OP) also.

Glass

I went to him for half an hour
As pure woman, pure misery
Fragile glass, breaking
Crumbling...
The house was silent in the heat
Only the old rafters creaking
He drew me to him
Rudely
With a lover's haste, an armful
Of splinters, designed to hurt and,
Pregnant with pain. Why
Did I
Not cry then, broken glass, beware?
Why did I not tell him then that
I no longer care
Whom I
Hurt with love and often without?
With a cheap toy's indifference
I enter other's
Lives, and
Make of every trap of lust.
A temporary home. On me, their
Strumming fingers may
Revive
The fond melodies of a past
I give a wrapping to their dreams,

27. A woman-voice
28. And a
29. Woman-small. I do not bother
30. To toll : I've misplaced a father
31. Somewhere, and I look
32. For him now everywhere.

A good number of Kamala Das's poems begin with the first person deictic pronoun "I". Most of these refer to her own "self" or to the aesthetic positions that she liked to represent. All the poems analysed so far have indicated that her poems translate a personal voice. From the preceding it is clear that it is up to the analyst to decide the nature of the utterance she is making. Since the surface meaning of what the "I" speaks cannot be taken seriously, constructing a context for the poem becomes necessary.

The title of the poem denotes a fragile transparent substance which presumably stands for the speaker's present mental construct and the experiences that caused fragility. From the larger context it could be discerned that insubstantial sex experiences and lack of freedom are the causes. The poem begins with the first person pronoun "I" followed by the verb "went" announcing that the utterance is going to be about the speaker's excursions to the landscapes of the male body, her desire to fuse with it and to know the pleasure of being. In the 32 lines of the poem "I", "my" or "me" appear twelve times. Third person references, that is, "he", "him", "they" and "their", are used eight times and there are four personal nouns. But unlike most of Kamala Das's poems, this one does not contain the second person pronoun "you". Further, there are two questions with apparently no listener to answer :

....Why
Did I
Not cry then, broken glass, beware?
Why did I not tell him then that
I no longer care
Whom I
Hurt with Love and often without?

These questions, directed to the speaker herself, speak of self-doubt. The discourse, therefore, is that of narration : the speaker narrating her on thoughts.

To create the context of isolation which is appropriate to the subject matter, Kamala Das alternatively makes use of nonfinite verbs such as "breaking", "hurt", "cry", "tell", "care" and "love". Specific qualities of these verb forms have been noted earlier. Another significant formal feature serving as an inlet to the poem's meaning is the rate of occurrence of the deictics of time and place. Hence the immediate location of the speaker is not clearly mentioned : the clause "The house was silent" (line five) means that she is referring to some house where she stayed in the past but it hardly indicates her present location. Again the time reference in the first line ("I went to him for half an hour") is unfixed, it could be psychological rather than historical. The tense system of the poem gives the impression that the speaker is reflecting on her emotions at the time of speech; she recalls the time when the incidents occurred which drove her to the present emotional situation.

Events that took place in the past are given in simple past in lines 1-11. Lines 11-17 tell about the conflict in the pleasure seeking protagonist's mind, which is the .result of the unhappy and even painful love affair. This tense sequence is broken in line 19 through the introduction of a verb in present simple denoting habitual action, "enter". But the object of the verb "enter" is "other's/Lives" which, taken literally, is a place where one cannot enter. On further examination it will be seen that this metaphoric expression is succeeded by a handful of similar aesthetically conjointed expressions. Thus :

> Make every trap of lust
> A temporary home. On me, their
> Strumming fingers may
> Revive
> The fond melodies of a past
> I give a wrapping to their dreams,
> A woman-voice
> And a
> Woman small.

These are the habitual actions the speaker performs and others perform in her. She finds momentary comfort and refuge in lust. By quenching another's lust, she makes pleasure which is a way to know herself. However, the seeming habitual actions are not what give her the pleasure she searches for — the continuity of pleasure rests in her ability to recreate those experiences in the effusive language of poetry.

The rest of the poem marks a remarkable shift in thought. The lines imply that the wanderings after lust do not fill in dearth. The last three lines show a deviation from the usual course of her search, and also from the course taken in this poem : she says that it is paternal love that she missed.

In "Ode to a Lynx" (CPI) the reader witnesses the consummation of the protagonist's approach to the production of pleasure as well as her evaluation of the men who participate in the process.

Ode to a Lynx

True, your leonine grace will impress
On any idle afternoon
Bring to mind the gold muscled flanks
Concealed by beige terrycot,
The deep armpits and the shadowed groin,
Exuding the musk of monsoon's inaugural shower,
Before I undress you mentally
I look once and then again,
I am obsessed with your mouth today,
The thin lips unveiling a short bitter smile,
A hemlock-smile that always discretion,
Or at other times, in a carnivorous rage, snarls
Oh lynx with piercing eyes,
I would hate to succumb to your charms,
Succumb as a yellow leaf does,
When the autumn-gales arrive.
If your desires were basics
Why did you pretend at all for three years

19. That you loved not me but my poetry?
20. Civilization irks me with its cunning ways.
21. I connect only with candour.
22. I have heard that every busy man seeks a womb,
23. A womb to hybernate in.
24. You thought you deserved a singing one.
25. With each pelvic thrust you hoped to hear,
26. In skilful verse, the rage of my response
27. Although with every cell awake in me I desire you
28. I shall not eddy to that inky depth again
29. Where I shall see, looking down
30. Not my familiar face but guilt's....

This poem, though captioned ''Ode to a Lynx'' is a deviation from the conventional ode. The subject matter of traditional odes is either public or private. The public is used for intensely personal and subjective which could either be meditative or reflective like Keats's ''Ode to a Nightingale.''[45] Kamala Das's ''Ode to a Lynx'' is an ode only in its celebration of purely personal and subjective context. The verse structure does not follow the pattern of any of the traditional odes.[46] Thus, it must be said that Kamala Das's ode is a ''free ode'' which violates the norms. Those formal features of the poem that explain its subject matter are examined in the following pages. The principal stylistic feature examined for this purpose is the employment of metaphors.

The poetic metaphor has the self generating capacity which generates ''radically fresh unpredictable tropes, each of which seems to produced a second, third and fourth buried inside the first.''[47] The truly creative metaphor is a speciality of poetic language where the poet uses it to rethink and reshape the world view. In studying the employment of metaphor in Kamala Das's ''Ode'' we will draw freely from Michael C. Haley's elucidation of the working of poetic metaphor.

The interplay between abstract and concrete, inanimate and animate, human and nonhuman is apparent throughout the poem. The metaphor part is rather a complex one with comparisons of man to a lynx (line 13), his smile to "hemlock" and the cumulative effect of all such comparisons to civilization (line 20). The smell that exudes from the man's groin is musky (line 6). This smell is further compared to the odour of earth on the commencing day of the monsoon rains. The sensation created by the musk smell of the lover's groin is contrasted with the sensation created by his "hemlock-smile" and lynx-like snarls. The musk is a sweet smelling substance produced in the glands of the musk deer. This offers fine contrast with the rage, the snarls and the piercing looks of the lynx which appear in lines 11-13. Out of this complexity grows an even more complex analogy in which all these constraints are reconstituted into "civilization".

The smell of the man's groin is likened to the odour of first *shower* of monsoon. The term *shower* is midway between abstract and concrete and so its function is not easy to explain. However, a noun like *shower* must be predictable of verbs like "fall" and "flow". But in a literal sense *shower* must not be predictable of shape or life or movement. In terms of what is predictable and what is not it is visualised as something that can exist. It could be further explained that the exuding musk of the groin which is likened to the inaugural shower which falls could also be falling or flowing seminal fluid. The creative potential of the first rains of monsoon runs parallel to the creative potential of semen.

The displacement of the man (represented by "you") by the beast (represented by "lynx") initiates tension between the human and non-human agents in the poem. The context indicates that Kamala Das is concerned with her own peculiar experience with a man who has hurt her feelings. For this reason, the "you" in the beginning of the poem seems to be working semantically as the predicate of the nonhuman. When man is predicated as lynx it is detached from its literal reference and reconstituted at a higher level of cognition, that is, the displacement of man to lynx moves it to a more generalised all encompassing sphere of animals, detaching the special feature 'human', thus making the noun 'man' psychospatially remote from the poet as an individual. By detaching man from 'human' the poet is in a way attempting to universalise her experience. The man's smile is a "hemlock smile" — where terms such as "sweet" "pleasant", or "innocent" would be the legitimate qualifiers, she uses the name of a poisonous plant which pushes him further down into the world of the inanimate. All these have been imaginatively compared to civilization (which irks the speaker!). Tension is at its crux when man is predicated to civilization which is man made and which is an abstract entity.

The general approach of users of a language is to identify the location of a noun belonging to a category on the grounds of that which could be predicated about them. The positioning of the noun *guilt* at the terminal position of the last line may be linguistically considered only as an abstraction. This abstraction is one that exists — the only literal predication we can make about it is that it exists. But *guilt* never exists in perceptual space, nor is it capable of movement. Thus, "guilt's (face)" is a figurative expression. The term "inky depth" — though archaic in tone — connotes space but space of a very different nature since it is not physically detectable. Hence, "inky depth" is another abstraction where "guilt's (face)" reflects. In this way the metaphors in this poem "can be described as the analogy by which the human mind explores the universe of quality and charts the non-measurable world."[48]

Beginning with the images of naked human body, shower and lynx the poet's mind visibly moves towards pure abstraction without the loss of concreteness. The term *guilt* in the terminal position of the last line has been brought to light by the imagery. It is apparent that the speaker has not been turned loose not very much by unlimited desire for sexual pleasure as by her own sensitivity to the perceptual images and the figurative projection of her own experience into them. This discussion has already revealed how this projection takes place linguistically. The discussion, thus, has captured some of the unleased feelings by reference to the linguistic categories to which those images belong.

Dreams and hallucinations also form part of the work of a writer who feels the need to find metaphorical equivalents for her thoughts. When Kamala Das depicts the hallucinations of her persona in "Woman without Her Shadow" (CPI) the reader feels the presence of the strange, the uncanny and the sinister.

Woman Without Her Shadow

She lay still, her open eyes two cartwheels
Stunned to a sudden halt. It seemed to her
At times that years had sped by since she had
Despatched her shadow to him who needed
Her, though she was older by years, and ill.
One day at last it returned, and raising
Herself from her pillow she cried, you have
Changed, I would not have recongnized you, had
I met you outside my home, you are dark,
Toasted black, as though some hell-fire had clasped
You to its bosom for a while. It replied
Smiling, I was busy, I had no time
To breathe. I walked along the streets at dusk,
Holding his hand in mine and sipped coffee
In South Indian cafes where each waiter
Who served us looked like another Jidoo
Krishnamurthy, and lay against him all
Through the winter nights; like a flag hoisted
On a mountain range till then unclaimed,
Unseen was my cheek against his,
And my heart against his, yet, I kept him
Yours for a spell and now I return,
Longing for home and rest. Planets slid like
Dice from player's hands, hurtling into space;
Their silence boomed in her ears. She ran down
The fearsome stairways of the sea. Like
A wild Westerly suddenly set free
She moved with a terrible ease, and in
The musty bracken of the sky the witch
Azaleas bloomed for her

31. And the unnamed birds of every heaven
32. Burst into song; there was then no disputing
33. Her strength or her legitimate role
34. But, from another city, lonelier
35. Than hers, he moaned in afternoon sleep,
36. Dreaming once again of her dying day...

As the caption indicates the poem is about the speaker and her shadow, the shadow being a particular means of poetic expression. The shadow, used as a trope, shows the poet's own narcissist preoccupation, wish fulfilment, and vision of death.

James G. Frazer in his *The Golden Bough* says that in older cultures the civilized man regarded his shadow or reflection as his soul or as a vital part of himself and if the shadow is detached from him he feared that he would die.[49] Otto Rank states that in present day cultures reflections and shadows are factors that remind the individual his mortality and more than that the announcer of death itself.[50] However, for Freud, the shadow or the double was a means of self-analysis.[51] The shadow image which marks a point of departure in Kamala Das's usual pattern of imagery is, however, related to the sun imagery which is recurrent in her. This is so because with sun exists shadow. In this poem, she uses this image to give vent to her passions and fears. She makes the shadow an equivalent of herself and thus identifies herself with the noncorporeal. The underlying idea might be to dramatise the attraction and repulsion between self and others, which, at the same time is a mark of failure to achieve full identity and the corresponding death instinct. The shadow — the imaginary self — could also be the projection of that part of the self which beckons death.

The poem is narrated in third person; however the "she" in this poem is none other than the "I" in the rest. The speaker says that she had once despatched her shadow, to her lover who was younger in age. This liberating of the shadow, the despatching of it and the conversation with it on its return denote finding a detached self and talking with one's own doppelganger. Existence as a shadow represents that part of the self of the artist which lives not in the real but in the illusory world, finding pleasure in the search for the absent. It is curious to note that the shadow's detachment, its touching and lying with another are equal to inviting death according to what Frazer says : "if (the shadow is) trampled upon, struck or stabbed (the individual) will feel the injury as if it were done to his person; and if it is detached from him entirely (as he believes that it may be) he will die."[52] Further if the shadow is touched by the shadow of another, it will, according to Frazer, yield hazardous results.[53] Thus, the quest for pleasure represented in this poem has terrifying effects.

The shadow in this poem, on another plane, could be viewed as an attempt to depersonalize and alienate the self; Kamala Das seems to make it a part of her speaker's ego. The woman, as seen in all the poems discussed so far, is a searcher of pleasure. In this poem's context she is revisiting her past carnal hungers and the affair with a young man as if every thing has been and are hallucinatory. The literary value of the despatching of the shadow and thus becoming a shadowless being lies in the creation of the surrealistic imagery that contain the thought. The surrealistic images of lines 10 and 23-32 evoke the feeling of uncanniness.

The commonplace subject matter and the simple imagery of the shadow's talk in lines 12-23 are sharply contrasted in the nine lines after that. After the exchange with the shadow the world is pictured as being remote, sinister and uncanny :

> Planets slid like
> Dice from player's hands, hurtling into space;
> ....Like
> A wild Westerly suddenly set free
> She moved with terrible ease, and in
> The musty bracken of the sky the witch
> Azaleas bloomed for her

The literary representation of the sense of estrangement the speaker is subjected to is apparent here. The shadow representing the particular psychological state of the speaker is thus given an extension in the surrealistic imagery of the lines quoted above.

Shadow, in the poem's context, is spirit detached from reality, a condition that creates uncanniness. It is a negative image which replaces the real self in the self's attempts to establish its identity through pleasure. However, it signals death-in-life too. The failure to gain real pleasure and the resultant suicidal drive into "The fearsome stairways of the sea" are the main impulses the thirty six lines of the poem carry.

The poem "White Man with Whiter Legs" (CPI) is an 'epilogue' to our analyses in this chapter as well as to Kamala Das's poetic rendering of her quest for identity and her existential approach to pleasure.

White Man with Whiter Legs

1. We learn from our surroundings as animals do or birds for
2. Our copyings we are not to be blamed. Our city crushes
3. Its inhabitants one by one and with urban finesse eats
4. Them, and afterwards sits facing the moon picking its teeth while
5. The fetor of its breath fills our mottled lungs at night. We ate
6. Our forefathers to gather the vigour for living. Later
7. Our descendants shall perhaps eat us when their turn arrives. No,
8. We shall not be surprised, we are ordinary, no God seems
9. Too keen to preserve us. We mated like Gods, but begot
10. Only our slayers. Each mother suckles her own enemy
11. And hate is first nurtured at her gentle breast and each man's seed
12. Is pregnant with his death. We are common, like some currency
13. Devalued we have a complex about our own shabbiness,
14. We are little wrecks at the basement of the sea, one Wreck
15. Examining the other with a faultfinding eye. The salt

16. Of our tears and of our blood, came from the sea, this is a world
17. Pickled well in brine, a world, we intend to save for a rainy day.
18. The sea does not spill over though there are no walls between
19. It and the earth. The houses stand where we store ourwealth. At times
20. A storm sinks some ships or a quick typhoon devastates a town
21. But nature aware of life's intent does not care to seek
22. Anyone's pardon, it sees no difference between the living
23. And the dead. Through a corpse's eye glazed to a visor death peers
24. Out at the living. At least it lives on to cool, to rot and
25. Fill the hollows with fat maggots that sprout like toad stools with out
26. Notice. On the epitaphs at graves lichen grows the fastest
27. As do scabs on wounds, yes, death promotes a kind of life. Who can say
28. For certain that we are superior to the maggots that
29. Eat us in the end? We are aided by death in our careers
30. We ought to learn to take in each sight filtered through its eye, for
31. At night the hunter and the hunted often lie asleep in
32. An innocence shared unwittingly and all the hatreds seem
33. Fancied, the prejudices unreal, what is real is what
34. We see, the child following a woodduck's trail, a woman's face
35. Peeping through tangled cloths lines, a starched face with a pudgy nose

36. The dark young woods that separate my home state from Karnataka,
37. The bewitched Muthanga forest flecked with the green glitter of
38. Eyes where the proud cheetah crossed our path and forget to stop and black
39. Monkeys with flywhisk tails jabbered in fear. In the remoteness
40. Of sleep I gathered a harvest for my eyes. Oh white man with
41. Whiter legs, luminous in the blue, have I met you in real
42. Life too, or are you just a symbol? The sky is a bazaar
43. At four a. m., crowded with the frosty faces of the stars,
44. It seems a happy place to land on, but a sunny porch and
45. My husband beside me, alive, that is all I shall ask
46. For, I shall retire from youth without a murmur, fold up
47. My lust neatly like a wedding grown, put it away for good
48. And keep my dreams' gate always shut although by God, he was so
49. Beautiful, white man with whiter legs
50. So luminous against the blue....

The poem's imagery candidly presents a view point which is the result of years' experience and observation. Whether the speaker would change the view in some other piece is overlooked. The deliberations of this poem are taken for granted as far as the purpose of this chapter is concerned. How the poem's imagery prepares the ground for the mature declaration in the closing lines of the poem is examined in the following pages.

The paramount importance of imagery, in particular that of metaphor, has been recognised by writers and critics from Aristotle on. Aristotle had maintained that 'to have a command over metaphor is the mark of genius.'[54] The transformational approach to metaphor can account for the "nature of reality and language by providing insight into how language is a reflection of an individual's reality".[55] A similar view is adopted in the analysis of the poem "Ode to a Lynx". The present piece shows an excess use of images. This necessitates a study of the employment of images in the poem.

In "White Man with Whiter Legs" Kamala Das's speaker attempts to effect a change in her approach to life. The patterns of images, metaphors and similes in particular, point to this end. She uses metaphors to impart human features to the nonhuman and to take away human features from the human, in order to depict the chaotic state of affairs compelling her free herself from entanglements.

The first line of the poem contains a simple simile, a comparison of the learning process of human beings with that of animals. The movement initiated by the figurative language of this simile is from human to nonhuman, that is, from "we" to "animals". In lines 2-4 we have the metaphorical statement "Our city crushes/ Its inhabitants one by one and with urban finesse eats / Them." Here the subject noun phrase "our city" is inanimate and the predicate "crushes its inhabitants" has the verb "crushes" that requires an animate agent. Here the inanimate "city" is attributed the qualities of a destructive beast. According to our intuition the term "city" is a substitute for the abstract noun "civilization" and hence what eats the human beings is their own civilization. In other words the speaker cautions the readers of the bestiality of modern civilization.

Introducing specificity to the agents of action in line 5, the poet introduces the improbable action — eating up "forefathers" — to give extension to the metaphor in lines 2-4. This attribution is further extended to the descendents in line 7. In line 9 there is shift from bestiality to divinity when referring to procreation. Here "we" (human) is equated to "Gods" (super human). However, the effect of this simile is counterbalanced in line 10 where the result of the superhuman action is given as begetting of "slayers". In line 10, again, there is an ironic paradox in

"Each mother suckles her own enemy". This is carried on to line 11-12 where each man's "seed" is described to be "pregnant with his death". The cumulative meaning of the images in lines 1-12 is that modern human world is no better than the world of spiders and scorpions where eating parents is the rule.

In lines 12-13 the movement from human to nonhuman is apparent in the comparison of a human feeling with a devalued currency. This takes us to lines 16-17 where there is the metaphor "this is a world/Pickled well in brine". Since pickling is a process of preserving food for future use, the world that is time, space and life when brought to the inanimate means corruption. Thus in most cases the metaphors move human qualities towards either the bestial or the inanimate. Hence, in order to create an effect of dissolution and decay of social order the poet uses metaphors that draw the inanimate objects, beasts and abstraction towards human or moves the human towards the other categories. All this is done to provide background to the protagonist's changed attitude to love and life.

Lines between 20 and 33 have a number of images depicting the speaker's mood. For example,

> Who can say
> For certain that we are superior to the maggots that
> Eat us in the end?

These lines, though they echo Hamlet, are not impressive. The images between lines 20-33 are trite and, therefore we do not attempt their analysis here. However lines 34, 37, 38, 42, 43, 46 and 47 have the poem's most effective images evoking sensuosity and stirring thought which are an antithesis to lines 1-33. The following are the metaphors that make the last part of the poem significant.

> The child following a woodducks trail (line 34)
> the bewitched Muthanga forest flecked with the green glitter.... (line 37)
> The sky is a bazaar / At four a. m., (lines 42-3)
> I shall retire from my youth without a murmur, fold up
> My lust neatly like a wedding gown.... (lines 46-7)

The last lines which mark the climax constitute the most significant part of this poem. Here the imagery displaces lust from human feature and draws it towards a material, "wedding gown". Those features that lead to this final image contrast with the overall imagery of the first thirty three lines. This offers conflict at the metaphorical level thereby giving the reader an aesthetic experience. It is as if the poet has understood the state of affairs and has found a way out. The too frequent use of metaphors allows the reader to understand the position taken by the poet. The seeming loss of identity in a chaotic world is a means of realizing the necessity to disentangle the self from the nerve shattering endeavours and to put it into a calm and enervating state of being able to enjoy sensuosity offered by Nature. From the generality of the images of the beginning the poem progresses to specificity where the woman speaker speaks of her own sensory experiences, about her place in the world and her own convictions about the future.

To sum up, the introductory part of this Chapter deals with the various aspects related to the subject matter and language of Kamala Das's poetry. This part drives home the fact that Kamala Das is a practitioner of what Mukařovský calls 'autostylization', or, in other words, through her poetry she challenges the existing social norms and hence 'aggressive'. The detailed examination of poetic syntax, lexis, pragmatic and other related aspects, use of reprtition, parallelism and tropes reveal that in Kamala Das's poetry the aggressive assertion of individuality and quest for pleasure appear simultaneously. Though some of the formal features appear in more than one poem, shift in thought is always accompanied by shift in style. In a nutshell, it is seen that the individuality projected thus is inseparable from Kamala Das's artistry.

Notes

1. Jan Mukařovský, *The Word and the Verbal Art*, trans. John Burbank and Peter Steiner (New Haven and London : Yale UP, 1977) 143.
2. Mukařoský, *The Word* 146.
3. See Mukařovský, *The Word* 146-7.
4. C.F. Mukařovský, *The Word* 158.
5. James S. Hans, "Presence and Absence in Modern Poetry," *Criticism* 22, 4 (1980) : 331.

6. Madhao B. Achwal, "The Literary Aspect of Obscenity", *The Roots of Obscenity,* ed. A.B. Shah (Bombay : Lalvani Publishing House, 1968) 32.
7. Michel Foucault, *The History of Sexuality Vol. I : An Introduction,* trans. Robert Hurley (New York : Random House, 1978) 73.
8. Foucault 105-106.
9. Foucault 147.
10. Eleanor Kuykendall, "Breaking the Double Binds", *Language and Style* 13, 4 (1980) : 81-93.
11. Robin *Lakoff, Language and Women's place* (New York : Harper Colpohon, 1975) 41-62.
12. Kuykendall 86.
13. O.N.V. Kurup, a Malayalam poet of renown (personal communication).
14. See Linda Anderson, "At the Threshold of the Self : Woman and Autobiography," *Women's Writings : A Theory,* ed. Moira Monteith (Sussex : The Harvester Press, 1986) 59.
15. Anderson 59-60.
16. Extension of syntax of one line to the following line.
17. See William A. Bennet, "Linguistics and the Evaluation of poetic Style", *Journal of Literary Semantics* 10, 2 (1981) 96.
18. For a detailed discussion see Bennet 95-103.
19. For a consideration see John B. Alphonso Karkala, "Gita Govinda' and 'Song of Solomon',". *Indian Literature* 28, 3 (1985) 95-102.
20. See Sukumari Bhattacharji, "A Survey of Sataka Poetry", *Indian Literature* 23, 5 (1980) : 27.
21. Bhattacharji 24.
22. Asyndeton is a rhetorical device where conjunctions and articles are omitted for effecting speed and economy.
23. See Richard D. Cureton, " "E.E. Cummings" A Case Study of Iconic Syntax," *Language and Style* 14, 3 (1981) : 203.
24. Repetition of conjunctions like 'and'.
25. See Jack J. Spector, *The Aesthetics of Freud : A study in Psychoanalysis and Art* (London : The Penguin Press 1972) 89.
26. Spector 94.
27. Spector 95.
28. John Milstead, " "Concrete" and "Abstract" as Stylistic Descriptors", *Language and Style* 16, 3 (1983) : 289.
29. Milstead 290.
30. Milstead 291.
31. Searle 66.
32. See E.L. Epstein, "Non-restrictive Modifiers : Poetic Features of Language", *Studies in English Linguistics ed.* Sydney Greenbaum (London : Longman, 1979) 221-234.
33. Epstein 226.

34. Ullmann, *Meaning* 74-77.
35. A linguistic item referring back to some previously expressed unit or meaning.
36. Taking up again a figure of speech which contains a repetition of words after other words have come between them.
37. See James Perrin Warren, " 'The Free Growth of Metrical Laws' : Syntactic parallelisms in 'Song of Myself'," *Style* 18, 1 (1984) : 31.
38. Barbara Herrnstein Smith, *Poetic Closure : A Study of How Poems End* (Chicago : University of Chicago Press, 1968) 98-99.
39. See S.J. Keyser, "Wallace Stevens : From and Meaning in Four poems," *Esays in Modern Stylistics,* ed. Donald C. Free man (London : Methuen, 1981) 101. The stylistic analysis of "Luminol" is based on this study.
40. See Fritz Blackwell, "Krishna Motifs in the poetry of Sarojini Naidu and Kamala Das," *Journal of South Asian Literature* 13- 1-4 (1977) : 12.
41. Blackwell 13.
42. Passage from Boileu's *Art Poetique* quoted by Ullmann, *Meaning* 50.
43. Cureton 183.
44. C.F. Martin Heidegger, *Being and Time,* trans. John Macquarrie and Edward Robinson (New York : Harper and Row, 1962) 307.
45. J.A. Cuddon, *A Dictionary of Literary Terms* (Delhi : Clarion Books, 1980) 460.
46. The traditional (Pindaric) ode is characterised by its division into strophe, antistrophe and epode and the Horation ode by its stanzaic regularity and metrical patterns.
47. See Michael C. Haley, "Concrete Abstraction : The Linguistic Universe of Metaphor," Ching, Haley, and Lunsford 141.
48. J.M. Murry, *Countries of the Mind* (Freeport, N.Y. : Books for Libraries Press, 1968) 9.
49. James G. Frazer, *The Golden Bough : A Study in Magic and Religion* (1922; New York : Macmillan, 1943) 189-92.
50. Otto Rank, *Beyond Psychology* (1941; New York : Dover, 1958) 76.
51. Sigmond Freud, *Collected Papers,* IV (London : Hogarth, 1925) 308.
52. Frazer 189.
53. Frazer 190.
54. Ullmann, *Meaning* 44.
55. Ronald F. Lunsford, "Byron's Spatial Metaphor : A Psycholinguistic Approach," Ching, Haley, and Lunsford 157.

4

The Dialectics of Individuality and Universality

The literature of a nation is a suprapersonal flow in which the single individual forms its accidental vehicle. The impetus that drives the literary personality is the national literature itself along with those from outside and other sociocultural aspects. The writer's inherent dispositions interacting with the external factors results in his participation in the suprapersonal developmental flow in literature.[1] In this way the writer determines literary development and is at the same time determined by it.

The developmental relation among writers (belonging, for example, to a school like that of the confessional) is a negation of individual uniqueness, but in reality it is an expression and consequence of it.[2] A writer of spontaneous emotional expression with a capacity to dominate over others in that mode becomes a significant personality influencing the rest. Personalities coverage in some aspects and diverage in others. Hence, individual writers have definite places in the suprapersonal development, that is, the school.

The relationship between writer and society reflects views of the society to which he/she belongs. Through the work the author is connected to the social milieu and in many cases he/she may be a defender of the milieu. The writer can also act through the work to raise the consciousness of the people in whose name the creation is done. This takes us to the dialectical presence of search for identity and the concern for the suffering or universal love in his/her poetry. In the case of a writer who takes his/her own life as theme the individual mark of style gains importance since the explicit self references using first person is intensified by the self referential value of the linguistic lay out itself. The autobiography presents the past experiences of the writer with respect to the present. The style of autobiography "No matter how doubtful the factors are related.... will at least present an "authentic" image of the man who "held the pen."[3] Expression proceeds from experience and language gives it shape through tropes and allied devices. An autobiographical work that contains confessions is the result of significant change that occurred in the poet's life. Past incidents might have affected change in the life of the speaker who describes not only what happened to him or her at different periods in life but also what he or she presently is. Linguistic deviation of the work might signify both deviation of time and identity.[4]

The use of first person "I" which remains all through the self revealing work (although not constantly), embodies both the present reflection and the multiplicity of the past states. Deviation in identity depicted by the style of the work is brought by the change in time. Hence the past "I" is not in its totality the present "I". In the statements made in the text and in their tone reflect the distance between the past and the present. The tone might express the feeling of what has been lost or what is sought. When the protagonist lives in a time of torturous present, she takes refuge in the soothing realm of the past. On the other hand for the poet the present might be the time of repose, recollecting the former tribulations. However, the speaker is not always a simple "I", as the constant use of this pronoun might make the poem less challenging and less exploratory.

Kamala Das's poems may have similarities with the poems of the American confessional poets like Sylvia Plath and Anne Sexton. But similarity is no sign of influence and in this study no attempt is made to place Kamala Das among the American confessional poets like Anne Sexton whose name has almost become synonymous with the genre. A brief note on confessionalism is not altogether out of place, although Kamala Das is not a wholly confessional poet.

Confessionalism has become known to the reading public as

a genre after Robert Lowell, W.D. Snodgrass, Anne Sexton and Sylvia Plath. The poetry of these writers is typically American, a product of an age of distress. Then there are writers like Donald Davie for whom confessional poetry is a "product of Romantic emphasis on the individuality of the poet."[5] And if we go back further we will see that many of those poets from D.H. Lawrence to Elizabeth Browning, Thomas Hood to Shakespeare, and even Sappho and Catullus had been confessional poets.

Laurence Lerner distinguishes the following characteristics of confession : factual accuracy of remembering, self-centeredness, self-abasement expressed in cliches, with none of the characteristics of poetry.[6] Confession is something that may cause shame in the individual who confesses; confessional poetry deals with intensely private experience (and therefore) deeply painful to bring into public. However, the shame itself being a universal experience the poet gains the courage to bear it. Shakespeare's persona in his Sonnets, though in the guise of a rhetorical strategy, admits the shame involved in depicting the union of lovers. Elizabeth Browning's *Sonnet's from the Portuguese* privately printed in 1842 contains forty four love poems addressed to her husband, all of them depicting her passion for him. Similarly D.H. Lawrence's "Mutilation" confesses his love for Frieda.

Hence, confessional poetry is not a modern phenomenon sprung in America. It existed in the past in one guise or the other. Further, confession alone is not poetry, it should have lyrical qualities also if it should be recognized as poetry. Here, Kamala Das's poetry is not viewed from the confessional angle and so no attempt will be made to compare her poetic work with Anne Sexton's or Sylvia Plath's. In the third chapter, our attempt was to show using stylistic tools that Kamala Das is an Indian writing in English with an aesthetic orientation. Therefore, a passing reference to how she could be viewed from the feminist perspective is necessary to the sort of treatment in this chapter.

A woman writer's creativity is often adversely influenced by the norms of the society. This constraint is worth mentioning in a study such as this. Susan Bassnet, while expressing her views about women's writings holds that history has created the impression that they are inferior to men. She observes : "...women are historically handicapped by having to operate within a system devised by men and in this predicament the very words with which they seek to articulate their marginality can only reinforce it.''[7] However the recent recognition of women's literary potentials have resulted in the breaking of the ``silence'' and in a polarisation between male and female writers. The popularisation of ``feminist'' writings where the first person account of women's sexual encounters, description of the plight of the socially oppressed women and description of the private lives of women have made this polarisation almost complete. However, these literary attempts have been called ephemeral as opposed to the depth and transcendence of male writings. Yet, the achievements of woman writers in socialist nations — Akhmatova of Soviet Union, for example, testifies to the fact that the literary potentials of women equal that of men and suppression and polarisation are the features of certain societies.

Kamala Das, while seeking to establish an identity of her own, expresses her concern for the women in general. When she published her first volume in 1965 and the second in 1967 the women's movement was still at its infancy. In the early seventies when she published her third volume the movement was still only a child. So whatever is said about the plight of women in those three volumes need not be the outcome of a direct influence of the movement. Rather she may be, after taking the cue from the movement, talking about her own views of women's condition in the contemporary society. As we have noted else where, her poems explore not only the self but also the universal experience of women. These explorations go beyond the limits of feminism — while exploring the problem of the women her poems embrace the problems of humanity in general. In what follows twenty poems (five hundred and twelve lines) are analysed. The analyses highlight the style features which explain the dialectics of individuality and universality. ``Without a Pause'' (SC), a poem that contains both purpose and vision of Kamala Das as a poet will provide the necessary setting.

Without a Pause

1. A baby-pink telegram reports
2. A loss, but don't oh, don't stop to think

3. Of a smile now gone, a favour left
4. Undone, but write, write, write without
5. A pause, while beyond the bolted door
6. Life crouches, a skeletal wild-eyed
7. Cat, but in these rooms, there is no sound,
8. No motion but that of this pen. On
9. This paper, so bridal white, write of
10. Life's purity, of life's betrayals....
11. Write of seed's first awareness, of
12. Children's malice, of adult love, of
13. Darkened rooms, where the old sit thinking,
14. Filled with vaporous fear. Write without
15. A pause, don't search for pretty words which
16. Dilute the truth, but write in haste, of
17. Everything perceived, and known, and loved...

The first reading of the poem reveals that the poet is speaking about her solitude, what life means to her and how and why she writers. As the first four lines state, poetry to her is a means to fill the vacuum in her mind. While doing so she is able to make the reader participate in the rituals of her poetic world. The aspects which enable the reader participate in the world of this poem are imagery, repetition, compounding and asyndeton.

Stephen Ullmann, quoting the French writer Ch. Bruneau says that poets as image makers belong to two classes : the "chemists" and the "inspired" type.[8] Poets like Rimbaud and Appollinaire who express themselves in "irrational" or "visionary" imagery belong to the class "inspired". Intellectual poets like Valery and Mallarme come under the other class. This classification seems to be applicable to Kamala Das also — she is rather an "inspired" poet than a "chemist". The last four lines of this poem make this almost clear :

Write without
A pause, don't search for pretty words which
Dilute the truth but write in haste, of
Everything perceived, and known, and loved...

Repetition is a fundamental device of intensification. The exact verbal repetition goes with a tendency to give "resonance" to the poem with the production of phonological echo using consonance, alliteration and assonance : "of a smile now gone, a favour left/Undone, but write, write, write without/ A pause, while beyond the bolted door..." Immediate repetition or Epizeuxis ("Write, write...") and the irregular repetition of "life" and the phrase "without a pause" seem to contribute to the lyricism in the poem. The superfluity of the irregular reiteration in many of the lines along with asyndetic structure compress the language of the poem — the poet says much in little. This sort of creation of poetic intensity while making the poem a very good piece of art, throws light upon the artistry of the poet.

The repetition which is a means to create poetic intensity, is also an indication of poverty of poetic resource.[9] The frequent use of repetition in Kamala Das is a sign of this handicap; this may be a handicap of women writers in general. However repetition has its own "eloquence".[10] It must serve to underline rather than elaborate whatever message she conveys. The emotion of her poems — we have had ample examples — is conveyed with force using repetition. From the psychological angle repetition suggests impersonal feelings which in order to find an outlet strikes repeatedly on the walls of her linguistic resources. The disorderliness in the manner of repetition (lexical repetition in the case of "write" and "life" and the phrasal repetition of lines 11-13) may suggest spontaneity and exuberance. This is a feature of free repetition and in this respect it contrasts with the ceremonious syntactic parallelism. Style features like these explain the poet's thoughts; she is thinking about the relation of poetry to life.

It is with the compound word "baby-pink" that the poem begins. This is followed by "wild-eyed" in line 6 and "bridal-white" in line 9. Invention of new words by compounding, which Kamala Das does so frequently, is a definite way of the poet's exceeding the normal resources of language. The cognitive meaning of the three compoundings given above could have been rendered by expressions such as "pink coloured telegrammes", "wild cat" or "staring cat" and "pure white". Such paraphrase would reveal the degree of compression and economy which is achieved by compounding. Once again these style features show how Kamala Das visualizes life : it is terrific, wild, yet fascinating as it gives her the power to write poems.

Another important factor related to the use of compoundings in this poem is the way they present ideas in condensed form. Leech has the following to say about such creations : "If a new word is coined it implies the wish to recognise a concept of property which the language can so far only express by phrasal or clausal description".[11] Hence, a word created in this way is not just a paradigm added to the existing stock, it is rather the "condensed" form of an idea newly formed in the poet's mind. Hence, "bridal-white" adds new dimensions to her poetic attempts. The oddity of the compoundings is related to the general usefulness of the ideas they stand for. The strangeness as such is a foregrounding device making us aware of emotional situations which we rarely notice in our everyday life.

In the expression "Life crouches" which is part of the metaphor in lines 6-7 ("Life crouches, a skeletal wild-eyed / Cat...") "crouches" describes the action of the subject "life". The subject, however, is not the instigator of the action. Here a very important aspect related to the theme of the poem is brought to the fore through foregrounding : things that happen are not under the control of the speaker. These happenings, it is understood intuitively, are those unhappy events which provide subject matter for her poetry. The poem's tense system stands in testimony to this : all of the verbs are in present tense ("reports," "think", "write", "crouches" etc.). However, the absence of agentives shows that the poem does not describe an action that is going on or taking place. Thus, the absence of agents, that is, the subjects of the sentences in the poem not being the instigators of the action described by the descriptive verbs, is consistent with the presence of verbs in simple present. This means that the poet is reacting to events in a passive manner.

The first line of the poem "A baby-pink telegram reports" introduces the nature of things and how they happen in the temporal world. This is followed by the expression "don't stop to think" which indicates that things in the world are transitory in nature. The actions signified by the verbs are truths which are within the limits of time. However, the dearth of agents and the use of simple present tense show timelessness. The subject matter of the poem is, it should be remembered, closely related to the theme of composing poems depicting life's experiences. The linguistic situation however defines the world depicted by the poet — it is a world without agents, a world in which events are inevitable. Writing about the events witnessed and experienced is the transitory function of the poet.

Kamala Das's treatment of her own experiences will show subtle variations when subjected to close analysis. In a good number of her poems the self will be seen emerging with a spirit which is at first dimly and then luminously universal. Meaning in the poems taken for analysis in the rest of this chapter will show this : beginning with personal themes that embrace the nonpersonal the poet will gradually emerge with an all encompassing view of humanity. In "Lines Addressed to a Devadasi" (CPI) Kamala Das draws pictures of herself and the rest of the women on a typically South Indian canvas.

Lines Addressed to a Devadasi

1. Ultimately there comes a time
2. When all faces look alike
3. All voices sound similar
4. And trees and lakes and mountains
5. Appear to bear a common signature.
6. It is then that you walk past your friends
7. And not recognize
8. And hear their questions but pick
9. No meaning out of words
10. It is then that your desire cease
11. And a homesickness begins
12. And you sit on the temple steps
13. A silent Devadasi, lovelorn
14. And aware of her destiny...

In this short poem Kamala Das uses co-ordinate structure for thematic effects. Using the polysyndetic structure[12] Kamala Das presents the changes brought by time on her speaker's outlook. She begins the poem with an adverb "ultimately" to indicate that the effect described is wrought by time. The conjointed words in line four connects objects of nature with human beings in relation to the changes wrought by time. The movement of the verse is closely related to the structure of the syntax. The rhythm created by coordination thus conveys the emotional state of the speaker.

The tittle of the poem refers to the poem's speaker as an addresser and the "devadasi" the third person addressee. This, needless to say, indicates the presence of another individual in the poem. However, it is evident that the "devadasi" is an alterego of the speaker on one side and a symbol of Indian womanhood on the other. A devadasi is a dredge of the society, her fate is nobody's concern.[13] If the speaker pictures herself as a devadasi, the cause should be utter hopelessness. And if the devadasi is a symbol, it points to something serious : It may mean that in the poet's view human culture is a disgusting waste product.

The first line of the poem "Ultimately there comes a time" is an indicator to the future which announces that the poem is going to be reflective. The remaining lines tell about the fate of the addressee — the "you" that appears in line 6 and 12. The only third person reference is "Devadsi" which appears in the line before the last. But unlike most of the poems discussed in the previous chapter there are no speech acts such as questions and commands. Thus, pragmatically the addressee is not in any more capacity than that of a mere listener. The addresser makes a series of statements, all of which are about her own feelings and judgements.

What is understood from the foregoing is that the speaker (the addresser) is reflecting on her own future. The verbs of sensation, movement and thought are all directed to this end. They appear in this sequence : "sound.... appear.... walk.... recognize.... Hear.... cease.... begins.... sit.... aware." It is a context of isolation that these verbs create as is appropriate to the subject matter.

The speaker's immediate location is not known, nor is there any reference to a particular point of time. Though future is implied in "there comes a time", this does not particularize time. This implies that time in this poem is psychological, not historical. Based on her past experiences and present state the speaker reflects upon her own future which through the allusion of the Devadasi is given a wider applicability — her fate is the fate of every woman sufferer. Thus the speaker is speculating on a probable future which appears to be inevitable.

The background which inspired Kamala Das to write a poem like the present one has been analysed in detail in the previous chapter. It is therefore felt that through the context the poet is producing an effect of the universal generalizability of an individual's experience.

It is seen that in the later poems of Kamala Das, that is, poems written after the publication of *The Old Playhouse and other Poems* there is little amount of erotica. Rather they deal with other deeply personal and universal themes. One might, therefore, feel that erotica has been a phase in the poet's life. The poem "The Snobs" (SC) is one of the earlier pieces that shows the interplay of personal emotions and concern for the plight of fellow beings.

The Snobs

1. Our house crouches in dust in the
2. Evenings, when the buffaloes tramp
3. Up the road, the weary herdsmen
4. Singing soft punjabi songs, and
5. Girls from free municipal schools
6. Pause shyly at our gate and smile.
7. What have I to offer them but
8. My smile, a half-dead, fraudulent
9. Thing, what have I to offer at
10. This shrine of peace, but my constant
11. Complaining voice? Forgive us. We
12. Are paltry creatures, utter snobs,
13. Who disowned our mothers only

14. Because their hands, we noticed, were
15. Work-worn, and, so to seek richer
16. Mothers and better addresses.
17. We must move on and on, until
18. We too, some day, by our children
19. May be disowed.

The poem "Without a Pause" with which the analyses in this chapter began has the expression "Life crouches" in the sixth line. "Life", which is an abstraction, is attributed animate quality in this case. "The Snobs" begins with an almost similar expression "Our house crouches" which has metaphorical value. The chief difference is that in the second case animate quality is attributed not to an abstraction but to an inanimate entity.

The first line of the poem shows movement from inanimate to animate. In lines 8-9 there is a counter movement — from animate (+human) to inanimate (smile — thing). In the first line an artifact is drawn towards the animate, since crouching is a distinctive characteristic of the category "animate". Hence, the house which is an artifact is brought to the animate.

The projection of the smile into the nonhuman "thing" suggests insincerity which foregrounds the theme namely the way of the world. However, in line 9 and in the succeeding lines Kamala Das pulls her speaker back towards the human :

....What have I to offer at
This shrine of peace, but my constant,
Complaining voice? Forgive us...

But she soon returns to dehumanisation in line 11-12 ("We / Are paltry creatures") and to categorization ("snobs"). But human feature is reinstated in the rest of the lines.

The setting, the location, is pictured as a dusty town and the time is an evening of the speaker's youth. The speaker is once again in a reflective mood. In other words she is recounting the way of the world of which she finds herself a part. The movement of the buffaloes and that of the girls and their shy smiles form part of the setting which constitutes the first stanza (lines 1-6). To this kinesthetic image is added the auditory image of the "soft

Punjabi songs''. The girls' shy smiles have overtones of warmness and expectation. The gracefulness of the things presented in this stanza is contrasted in the next : the ''shy smile'' with the ''half-dead fraudulent'' smile, and the soft music with the ''complaining voice.'' The second stanza thus pictures the ''other'' world, a malicious world of ''paltry creatures'' and ''snobs''.

Personal feelings are, in this way, found to attain universality in lines 7-9. The reference to those women who serve their children, but who are abandoned by them in old age is a powerful image picturing their plight. The prediction of what awaits those who belittle those who serve pure love concludes the poem. The meaning created has universal applicability : it explains the fate of those of the human race that have become excessively selfish.

The feeling of guilt of the existential speaker and the resultant suicidal impulse are treated in the poem ''The Suicide'' (DS). The feeling contained in the poem is the feeling of every alienated being, who is at the brink of losing her identity.

According to Martin Heidegger the self can recover its lost individuality — lost in the innumerable connections with others in the day to day affairs — by the fundamentally solitary act of individuality, that is, the capacity, to decide its own death. However, the alienation, or the feeling of distance between the self and others, leads the self, paradoxically, into sameness with others.[14] The self's modes of encountering others in the world of everyday dealings are ''domination'' and ''liberation''. The distance that the self maintains with the other is the cause of conflict between the self and the other.[15] In everyday dealings the tendency of the self is to dominate in interaction; in doing so the self forgets the freedom of the other and thus forget's its own freedom. In both cases — in domination and liberation the identity of the self is hampered, and it is in confronting death that the self comes into its individual being.

Death is a possibility confronting which requires overcoming of the most radical form of otherness and negativity. The ''impassioned freedom towards death''[16] gives the self ''unshakable joy''[17] thus converting the negative into positive. ''The Suicide'' seems to be an attempt at converting the suicidal urge into positive creativity.

The Suicide

Bereft of soul
My body shall be bare.
Bereft of body
My soul shall be bare.
Which would you rather have
O kind sea?
Which is more dead
Of the two?

I throw the bodies out,
I cannot stand their smell,
Only the souls may enter
The vortex of the sea.
Only the souls know how to sing
At the vortex of the sea.

Your body shall be dead,
Poor thing,
Dead as driftwood, drifting
And drifting to the shore.
Your body shall ride the tide,
Rider, slumped dead
On white war-horse,
Charging.

Your body shall bruise white
against the coral reefs,
Your body,
Your lonely body.

I tell you, sea,
I have enough courage to die,
But not enough
Not enough to disobey him
Who said : Do not die
And hurt me that certain way.

How easy your duties are.
How simple.
Only rear a hungry roar,

Leap forward,
And retreat.
You swing and you swing,
O sea, you play a child's game.

But,
I must pose,
I must pretend,
I must act the role
Of happy woman,
Happy wife.
I must keep the right distance
Between me and the high.
I must keep the right distance
Between me and the low.

O sea, I am fed up
I want to be simple
I want to be loved
And
If love is not to be had,
I want to be dead...

While I enter deeper,
With joy I discover
The sea's hostile cold
Is after all skin-deep.
The sea's inner chambers
are all very warm
There must be a sun slumbering
At the vortex of the sea.

O sea, I am happy swimming
Happy, happy, happy...
The only movement I know well
Is certainly the swim,
It comes naturally to me.

69. I had a house in Malabar
70. and a pale-green pond.
71. I did all my growing there
72. In the bright summer months.
73. I swam about and floated,
74. I lay speckled green and gold
75. In all the hours of the sun,
76. Until

77. My grandmother cried,
78. Darling, you must stop this bathing now.
79. You are much too big to play
80. Naked in the pond.

81. Yes, the only movement I really know
82. Is swimming,
83. It comes naturally to me.
84. The white man who offers
85. To help me forget,
86. The white man who offers
87. Himself as a stiff drink

88. Is for me,
89. To tell the truth,
90. Only water.
91. Only a pale-green pond
92. Glimmering in the sun.
93. In him I swim
94. All broken with longing.
95. In his robust blood I float
96. Drying off my tears.

97. Yet I can never forget
98. The only man who hurts.
99. The only one who seems to know
100. The only way to hurt.

101. Holding you is easy
102. Clutching at moving water,
103. I tell you, sea,
104. This is easy.

105. But to hold him for half a day
106. Was a difficult task.
107. It required drinks
108. To hold him down

109. To make him love.
110. But, when he did love,
111. Believe me,
112. All I could do was sob like a fool.

113. O sea,
114. You generous cow,
115. You and I are big flops
116. We are too sentimental
117. For our own
118. Good.

119. Lights are moving on the shore.
120. But I shall not return.

121. Sea, toss my body back
122. That he knew how to love.
123. Bereft of body
124. My soul shall be free.
125. Take in my naked soul
126. That he knew how to hurt.

127. Only the soul knows how to sing
128. At the vortex of the sea.

This poem has one hundred and twentyeight short verse-lines, irregular stanzaic pattern and occasional rhyme. Verbal repetition, parallelism and orchestration with various kinds of phonological echo — consonance, alliteration and assonance — pervade the whole of the poem. They express the thoughts of the speaker and the way of the world at large superabundantly. In a poet like Kamala Das, the need to express feelings being superabundant, repetition occurs as if in a ritual that employs a metapersonal language.

Basically free verse is based on syntactic patterns strengthened by parallelism and sound orchestration. Repetition is the fundamental constitutive principle of free verse. In free verse forms and interrelations are represented by verbal and thematic reiteration. In almost all the cases of verbal parallelism, the repetition of the individual words is accompanied by the repetition of the syntactic structure. Parallelism is that aspect of poetic language which relates poetry to music.[18] Alliteration, assonance and consonance (phonological parallelism) play an important part in making poetry musical. Alliteration is chiming; we are made to think of the possible connections between the two or more words due to the similarity of sound. However, it must also be noted that the connection is also made through the abstract ways of empathy and sinaesthesia. The use of apostrophe is another important stylisitc feature of the poem. The speaker addresses the sea — something that stands midway between abstract and concrete — eight times ("O sea" and "sea") in the poem, thus introducing contextual absurdity. Since the listener or the interlocutor in human communication should be human, the apostrophe attributes human qualities to an abstraction. The chief advantage in the use of apostrophe is that the poet can express her attitude to a person or thing with greater subtlety. This device, like the rhetorical question, is a conventional feature of elevated poetic language. The formal indicator of apostrophe in this poem is the vocative "O sea" (repeated five times).

On another plane talking to a non-human entity which is a cardinal feature of this poem is a violation of a selectional restriction.[19] The object of direct address must be human, or animate or human like. To violate this rule by addressing an inanimate entity as if it were a person is to invent an instance of personification, which is a figure of speech like the apostrophe. This 'figure' explains away the anomaly of addressing an inanimate entity. But the anomaly involved in asking the personified entity to do something or to hear a speech needs explanation. The explanation for this occurrence in "The Suicide" is the one we have given above, taking the address as an apostrophe.

The subject matter of the poem is dialectical : the experience is personal and at the same time universal. This is explained by the parallelistic structure and the relations that link difference with similarity (the nonparallel with the parallel). The awareness that something is terribly missing in the life of any ordinary mortal is thus formalised in this manner.

It is obvious that in most of the repetitions in this poem syntactic reiteration is accompanied by parallelistic effects at semantic and phonic levels. Claudio Guillen, following the Spanish writer Alarcos, distinguishes four kinds of rhythm in poetry : a sequence of sounds, a sequence of grammatical functions, a sequence of accented syllables and a sequence of psychological contents (feelings, images, etc.)[20] The poetic effect of a piece such as we are examining depends on the tension, interaction, or contrast among the parallelistic and non parallelistic units. The dialectic of sameness and diversity — the hermeneutic circle that affects the very notion of literature — is also found in the poem itself. How parallelism harmonizes expression of the same thought through either the repetition of the same idea in different words or counterposes two different thoughts or adds to the thought by means of a variant expression which is not purely repetitive, is illustrated.

Lines 1-4 :

Bereft of soul
My body shall be bare
Bereft of body
My soul shall be bare.

These lines, with which the poem opens illustrate what is said in the preceding paragraph. These syntactically parallel lines harmonise the expression of one thought the effect of which points at the present mental state of the poem's speaker.

Only the souls may enter
The vortex of the sea.
Only the souls know how to sing
At the vortes of the sea.

This syntactic reiteration is accompanied by parallelistic effects on semantic and phonological level. On the semantic plane, meaning is emphasized : the suicide by drowning in the sea. Alliteration of /s/ and /v/ and rhyme of /e:/ in lines 12 and 14 add to the literary aspects.

Lines 15, 19, 23 :

Your body shall be dead
....
Your body shall ride the tide
....
Your body shall bruise white

The syntactic reiteration echoes the psychological state of the speaker : visualizing death in its nakedness. Assonance of /ai/in line nineteen gives salience to the solitude of the speaker.

Lines 41-43, 46-49;

I must pose
I must pretend
I must act the role
....
I must keep the right distance
Between me and the high.
I must keep the right distance
Between me and the low.

The grammatical frame mimics the semantic frame : the act of reminding. The lyrical quality of the speaker's solitude and the tension is contained in the parallel statements. The sad and disconsolate state of mind of the speaker attains universal applicability in these lines because what is said about the speaker is the fate of every house wife in a normative society.

Lines 50-51, 55 :

I want to be simple
I want to be loved
....
I want to be dead
and

Lines 58-61 :

The sea's hostile cold
is after all skin deep
The sea's inner chambers
are all very warm

It was noted that poetic effect depends upon the tension, inter-action or contrast among the parallel and non-parallel units.

In the lines quoted above the dialectic of sameness and diversity is apparent. In lines 50, 51 and 55 the drift from line to line shows something like an intensification that sets off in different ways what was previously said. Line 51 is connected to 50 : it carries what is said in line 50, echoes it, defines it and is then contrasted in line 55.

In the following lines the occurrence of diphrasis (saying the same thing twice) which is not easily distinguished from parallelism in this context is apparent.

Lines 84 and 87 :

The white man who offers
....
The white man who offers

Lines 70 and 71 :

and a pale green pond
....
only a pale green pond

Lines 98-100

The only man who hurts
The only one who seems to know
The only way to hurt

Lines 122 and 126 :

That he knew how to love
....
That he knew how to hurt

The universality noticeable in the parallelistic structure of this poem may help establish that Kamala Das is not simply following the English verse pattern. The following verse lines belonging to both spatially and temporally remote cultures — Sumerian hymn and the Chinese *shiching (Book of Odes*) — will show similarities with the lines of Kamala Das :

1. Sumerian :

When bread had been toasted in the shrines of the land
When bread had been baked in the ovens of the land,
When heaven had been moved away from the earth,
When earth had been separated from heaven.

2. Chinese :

> Dry leaves, dry leaves,
> The wind tosses you about
> ....
> Dry leaves, dry leaves,
> The wind blows you along.[21]

Thus it is very much clear that the poem "The Suicide" contains a high amount of parallelism in which there is good amount of exact verbal repetition. The poem, as has been observed, is built around the theme of love and despair and has a typically dense atmosphere. It has the experience of solitude in its barest form to offer — the experience of celebrating one's own death which suggests a universal applicability in the suitable frame of parallelism and through the introduction of contextual absurdity. If this poem is capable of evoking 'pity and horror' it is hate for the male oppressor that finds formal equivalents in "Killing of the Chameleons" (SC).

Killing of the Chameleons

As child, he stoned a chameleon, killing
It and then wept into mother's hair giving
No reasons. No, it was not pity
That made him weep so, but his own cruelty,
A weapon just discovered. Even now his
Killings are all unintentional;
Each hurting word a stone that did not mean to
Kill, but killed all the same and each unkindness
A snake reared only to hiss,
But struck. He has handsome finger-nails, and small
Slanting eyes. He makes ladies who come to call
Wait, wait and fret for him for half
An hour, in verandah, under slow fans
Before he walks in, his heavy feet chomping
Long yards of uncarpeted floor,

16. And says with the most beguiling smile, darling
17. So sorry to keep you waiting.

The poem has seventeen long drawn out verse lines with no stanzaic division. It takes the form of a series of analogies : the male associate is compared successively to a chameleon-killer, a homicidal snake and a sadist of the sort.

In the first five lines a very familiar-pastoral image of Kerala related to boyhood is introduced with subtlety, to expose the wanton cruelty of men as opposed to the emotionally subtle women. A popular superstition associated to the chameleon is that it can suck blood from a child's navel from a distance. So it is a practice among the boys in the villages to stone this harmless reptile to death. Identifying herself with the chameleon and her man with the wanton killer the poet tries to universalize the pain. Indian women in general are victimes of beliefs. The chameleon-killler weeps (like the crocodile weeping after a kill) and hides himself in his mother's hair — when he grows he replaces the chameleon with a woman. The image of the hissing snake which is unitentionally homicidal is likened to the man who cuts with unkind words. The last of the images is a weak one : the man as a sadist who finds pleasure in making women wait for him "under slow fans".

The women sufferers are directly introduced in line 11 ("ladies, " and Indian English idiom meaning "women"), though their presence is felt throughout the poem. The cause of the sufferings — the men — is represented by the "he" which appears in the first line and subsequently in lines 5, 10, 11, 12 and 14. Thus, the all pervading male ego is represented by the third person pronoun "he" and is used a number of times before which the women represented by "ladies" is insignificant and appears only once. This is quite unlike the poems we analysed in the previous chapter where we noted the superabundance of personal pronouns representing the woman speaker.

The locale, in the beginning of the poem, is a typical Kerala village. This is shifted by the hypothetical imagery of a hissing snake (the "hiss" introducing an auditory image) which ultimately strikes. All of the verbs except those in lines 11 and 12 depict the actions of the male : "he stoned, " and "(he) wept" in lines 1 and 2, "He makes ladies....wait, " "he walks" in line 14 and "[he] says" in line 16.

The image of the deadly stone throw and the killer snake almost completely contain the story of the poem. However, in lines 11-17 the intensity with which the man is developed as a killer till line 10 is weakened with the introduction of "handsome finger nails" (line 10), "slanting eyes" (line 11) and the endearing address "darling" (line 16). Yet, "beguiling smile" in line 16 explains the deceptive element in the man's disposition. His chomping feet echoes (along with the suggestion of movement) haughtiness. These, however, do not match with the deadliness of the boy/man described in lines 1-10.

The poem is a 'murderous' analysis of the male character. The view is typically feminine and the poet has succeeded in bringing about the nature of the cruelty a middle class woman is subjected to in a male dominated society.

Nostalgia is an experience which, people are subjected to without exception. It is a feeling common to all (universal). Kamala Das's presentation of nostalgia in her poetry is mixed with loneliness, the mark of the existentialist. Expression of nostalgia in poetry may be an act of confession; it has some other meaning as well. "A Hot Noon in Malabar" (SC) is a poetic composition presenting nostalgia in a unique style. The poem has many beautiful images and has examples of proper lexical selection. Sound symbolism creates the relaxed mood proper for reflection.

A Hot Noon in Malabar

1. This is a noon for beggars with whining
2. Voices, a noon for men who come from hills,
3. With parrots in a cage and fortune-cards,
4. All stained with time, for brown Kurava girls
5. With old eyes, who read palms in light sing-song
6. Voices, for bangle sellers who spread
7. On the cool black floor those red and green and blue

8. Bangles, all covered with the dust of the roads,
9. For all of them, whose feet, devouring rough
10. Miles, grow cracks on the heels, so that when they
11. Clambered up our porch, the noise was grating,
12. Strange...This is a noon for strangers who part
13. The window-drapes and peep in, their hot eyes
14. Brimming with sun, not seeing a thing in
15. Shadowy rooms and turn away and look
16. So yearingly at the brick-ledged well. This
17. Is a noon for strangers with mistrust in
18. Their eyes, dark, silent ones who rarely speak
19. At all, so that when they speak, their voices
20. Run wild, like jungle-voices. Yes, this is
21. A noon for wild men, wild thoughts, wild love. To
22. Be here, far away, is a torture. Wild feet
23. Stirring up the dust, this hot noon, at my
24. Home in Malabar, and I so far away....

A concept which will be of use to study the patterning of sounds and their relation to the meaning of the poem is that of the "motif". Here "motif" is the recurrent combination of sounds. In a poetic passage a number of such motifs may combine, follow each other in succession or in irregular pattern, fuse together or may recur. There exists certain relationship between the words in the poem and the sounds with which they are constituted. In some situations the sounds themselves express the situation. From the first ten lines of the poem we take the following words which show sound linkages :

Lines :

1. "This is" : /ð/, /z/
2. "Voices," "hills" : /v/, /z/, /l/
3. "All", "Kurava girls" : /l/, /v/, /z/
4. "Old eyes", "palms", "light" : /l/, /z/
5. "Voices," "bangle-sellers" : /v/, /z/, /l/

6. "Cool black floor", "those", "blue" : /l/, /ð/
7. "Bangles, " "all", "roads" : /l/, /z/
8. "All ", "them", "whose", "devouring" : /l/, /ð/, / z/, /v/
9. "Miles", "heels", "that", "they" : /l/, /z/, /ð/

All the recurring motifs noted above are voiced consonants and have a relaxed articulation.[22] The deictic word "this" points to an immediate situation which is supported by the verb in present tense and the time adverbial "noon". At the abstract level of sound symbolism, the presence of the soft consonants symbolically represents the content : the half-dreamy, relaxed mood of the speaker.

The time — the noon — at which the speaker reflects her past experiences when at her home in Malabar in similar afternoons and what must be happening there presently is given emphasis by the repetition of "this". Further the placement of the word in the thematic position signals the present, the voiced consonant /ð/ initiates the role of sound symbolism in giving the poem its mood. Thus time and mood are represented by the first word itself. The voiced consonant /ð/ is followed by another, that is, /z/ in the same line and /v/ in the next.

While the motifs noted above support the realxed, reflective mood and create context, the imagery, as in the case of "Killing of the Chameleons" is related to the village life of Kerala. The tribal fortune tellers with caged parrots and cards, the palm-reading Kurava girls, the bangle sellers and the pedestrians exhausted under the summer sun looking for a well have the typical colour of the villages in Kerala. The expression "sing-song voices" while adding emphasis to the speech of the Kurava girls, forms part of the foregrounded vocabulary, "whining voices", "voices run wild" and "jungle voices". These sensory images are accompanied by the hypothetical imagery of the "wild men" initiating "wild thoughts" and "wild love" — it is as if she is "mixing memory and desire." The liquid consonant /l/ in "wild", "like", and "love" imparts softness to these lines.

tribal fortune tellers with caged parrots and cards, the palm-reading Kurava girls, the bangle sellers and the pedestrians exhausted under the summer sun looking for a well have the typical colour of the villages in Kerala. The expression "sing-song voices" While adding emphasis to the speech of the Kurava girls, forms part of the foregrounded vocabulary, "whining voices", "voices run wild" and "jungle voices". These sensory images are accompanied by the hypothetical imagery of the "wild men" initiating "wild thoughts" and "wild love" — it is as if she is "mixing memory and desire." The liquid consonant /l/ in "wild", "like", and "love" imparts softness to these lines.

As in the case of "Without a Pause", lexical compounding has an important function in this poem also. The five compoundings, ("fortune-cards," "bangle-sellers," "window-drapes", "brick-ledged" and "jungle voices") have each their role in the images of the poem — they help compress meaning. The last verbless clause "I so far away" which functions as a semi sentence gives final emphasis to the nostalgia developed through the poem's twenty four lines.

The immediate expression of an individual's feelings and emotions can make a verse composition a lyric. A childhood reminiscence would be a lyric if it is an immediate expression of emotion. But if such a poem is 'confessional', that is, if the poem is an exact rendering of the individual private experience, it is not lyric, not even poetry. So in order that an autobiographical or confessional poem acquire qualities peculiar to poetry the poet should add his or her imagination to the purely personal experience. In the preceding discussion it was noted that the poet had mixed images of memory and desire to create the desired aesthetic effect. The poet reshapes past experience in the language of poetry adding novelty to the mode in another piece titled "Punishment in Kindergarten" (SC).

Punishment in Kindergarten

1. Today the world is little more my own.
2. No need to remember the pain
3. A blue-frocked woman caused, throwing

4. Words at me like pots and pans, to drain
5. That honey coloured day of peace.
6. "Why don't you join the others, what
7. A peculiar child you are"!
8. On the lawn, in clusters, sat my school mates sipping
9. Sugar cane, they turned and laughed;
10. Children are funny things, they laugh
11. In mirth at other's tears, I buried
12. My face in the sun-warmed hedge
13. And smelt the flowers and the pain.
14. The words are muffled now, the laughing
15. Faces only blur. The years have
16. Sped along, stopping briefly
17. At beloved halts and moving
18. Sadly on. My mind has found
19. An adult peace. No need to remember
20. That picnic day when I lay hidden
21. By a hedge, watching the steel-white sun
22. Standing lonely in the sky.

Kamala Das has written quite a number of poems on remembered experience. Reminiscences of childhood form an expressive part of such poems. "Punishment in Kindergarten" has an apparently unimportant incident from childhood as its subject matter and in that vein it offers novelty of presentation. Instead of the usual way of glorification of childhood Kamala Das takes up the helplessness, dependency and lack of individuality of the childhood. Being an adult means possessing individuality and potential to create.

The childhood reminiscence found in English Romantic poetry is in every way a celebration of sentimentalism and innocence. Such a view is out of favour today. The autobiographical content of "Punishment in Kindergarten" relates it to the majority of the poems of Kamala Das, and the same element distinguishes the poem from "children are close to heaven" poems of the English

Romantics. An examination of the imagery in the poem would show why it stands out among the poems glorifying childhood. The images in the poem are not stereotyped, they belong to the everyday world. "The "blue-frocked" nun, the "honey-coloured day of peace" (such metaphors seem to be out of fashion today), the children sipping sugar cane and laughing, the solitary child burying her face in "sun-warmed" hedge and the "steel-white sun/ Standing lonely in the sky" are images depicting the world of perception. They express the emotions of one individual which could be universally shared.

The image of the "steel-white" sun, the furnace of creation, standing alone in the sky is all the more important. The sun, with its energy spread out, stands alone as the symbol of creation. The child imbued with artistic energy too is alone. Thus, this last image underlines the universality of artistic alienation.

The quotation in lines 6-7 gives a vivid picture of the experience. The gradual fading of its impact while the time passes is enacted in the slow moving temporal syntax of the following lines :

> The words are muffled now, the laughing
> Faces only blur. The years have
> Sped along, stopping briefly
> At beloved halts and moving
> Sadly on.

The tense pattern has to do with the shifting scenes : present tense sets the time of writing and past the time of experience.

Using incidents and experiences belonging to the past as subject for poetry open certain of the poems of Kamala Das to incoherence and fragmentation. Yet, this could be viewed as part of an effort to achieve wholeness. She writes about the past in order to attain individuality in the present. The past and the present, as we shall unfold in the analysis that follow, by turns, can be shadow and substance, the presence of each being reflected against the absence of the other. The interplay of tense should, therefore, be taken as a formal feature which purports the alternation of presence and absence. The present may seem unreal due to its ephemerality, or due to the absence of any worthwhile contact with the "real" internal world. This, *a priori*, results in frustration.

The memories might be substantial for the existential persona (speaker) in such poems because for her the past world she pictures (with the exception of the world in "Punishment in Kindergarten" and poems of similar nature) had substance in the past. The present is the absence of substance and therefore is shadowy.

The memory of her grandmother from whom she received love and who died when she was young, is an obsession for her. We will find the manifestation of this in "My Grandmother's House" (SC) and "Evening at Old Nalapat House" (CPI). In these poems the self is pictured as emerging with the absent grandmother.

My Grandmother's House

There is a house now far away where once
I received love... That women died,
The house withdrew into silence, snakes moved
Among books I was then too young
To, read, and, my blood turned cold like the moon
How often I think of going
There, to peer through the blind eyes of windows or
Just listen to the frozen air,
Or in wild despair, pick an armful of
Darkness to bring it here to lie
Behind my bedroom door like a brooding
Dog.... You cannot believe, darling
Can you, that I lived in such a house and
Was proud, and loved.... I who have lost
My way and beg now at stranger's doors to
Receive love, at least in small change?

In this poem the speaker says much in a few words : around one hundred and twenty words put in sixteen lines. A serious reading will reveal that the grandmother in the poem is a mother substitute. The desire to be under the care of the mother substitute and hence to be near to her could be the expression of the natural desire to be one with the mother, separation from whose womb subjects the self to uncanniness. Uncanniness, it is explained by writers like Heidegger, is the affective state in which the self finds itself, and is due to the self's encounter with the world, where it is all alone, and where it "discovers the sheer fact of existing."[23] Identifying oneself with the absent mother (mother substitute) is a unique experience fit for poetic subject matter; this explains the dialectics of absence. Images depicting the old house where Kamala Das's grandmother lived, the green pond in which the poet used to swim (Cf. "The Suicide"), the landscape and the surf breaking on the coral reef (Cf. "Composition") (DS) in the beach near her ancestral home suggest fullness of the distant and the absent and the emptiness of the near and the present. Hence, it is seen that the aesthetic form is structured around the absent.

The absence of the grandmother prompts the poet to search for the missing, which is the quest for identity too. The experience that forms the psychological background of "My Grandmother's House" is not confined to the poet alone. It is the experience of every woman who is forced to live in a similar atmosphere.

Deictic words such as "this", "now", and "here" denote proximity of objects and events to the speaker and "that ", "then" and "there" show lack of proximity. In poems dealing with remembered experience these words serve as useful clue to the interpretation of present and absent. Thus :

1. First and second person pronouns : I, my, you
2. Demonstrative : that
3. Adverbs of place : there, here
4. Adverbials of time : now, once, then.

These deictic expressions build the world within the poem.[24] Their role is apparent in the beginning of the poem itself : "*There* is a house *now* far away where once / *I* received love. *That* woman died,...Much of what the poet wants to communicate is carried by the deictic words. The opening lines quoted above are forceful because of the emotion contained in the language and the implied context. The lines pull the reader towards the scene of action, to the old house at a far away place where once she received love. The link between the house, the grandmother, the speaker and "love" is clearly brought forth in the opening lines.

The deictic words with their 'pointing' function have definite meaning. So is the definite article "the" which is used twice (in lines 3 and 5). The use of definite past as noticed in "That woman died/ The house withdrew into silence, snakes moved" is an indicator of definiteness of meaning. Had this line been in the past perfect tense it would have suggested vagueness. Here the preference for the past tense suggests narrative directness; vagueness in this case can create doubt about the truthfulness of the statements — the reader will doubt whether the persons ever lived or the incidents ever took place. Still, it should be realized that the inferred situation created by the poet with all these devices does not have to be under the rules of reason.

The poem uses variety of sound patterns, assonance, alliteration and consonance in particular. Parallelisms of this kind set up an equivalence[25] between two or more elements within the poem. Sound patterns like alliteration and assonance being external features, interpreting phonological equivalence of this sort involves the appreciation of some external connection between these elements. The alliterative structure of this poem is, as usual, a pattern mounted on the natural pattern of the language. This is one of the types of foregrounding which makes the poem more organised. The emotions of love and despair and the loneliness of the speaker is thus transferred to the reader through phonological foregrounding.

The above observation about the patterning of sound in the poem may take us to some other points. These patterns show the presence of conscious or unconscious artistry which accounts for the coherence of the message of the poem, though there is seeming incoherence in the surface structure. One significant quality of alliteration is that it may connect the lexical item which contain the repeated sound so that the readers are made to think that there exists a possible connection between the words. Thus, "silence" and "snakes", "despair" and "darkness", "bed-room" and "brooding" seem to be related to one another. The major sound patterns of the poem are as follows.

Consonance.

Line 1. house, once : /s/

2. house, silence : /s/
4. books, was : /z/
5. read, blood, cold; /d/
7. eyes, windows : /z/
8. listen, frozen : /n/
14. proud, loved : /d/
15. strangers, doors : /z/
16. receive, love : /v/

Assonance.

Line
1. house, now : /au/
3. house : /au/
11. bedroom, brooding : /u:/
14. proud, loved : /au/
14. I : /ai/
15. My : /ai/
16. receive, least /e:/

Alliteration

Line
1. where, once, women : /w/
3. silence, snakes /s/
5. my, moon : /m/
9. despair : /d/
10. darkness : /d/
11. behind, bedroom, brooding : /d/
12. dog, darling : /d/
10. bring : /b/
11. behind, bedroom, brooding : /b/
13. lived /l/
14. loved, lost : /l/
15. strangers : /s/
16. smell : /s/

While consonance and assonance create the drowsy sonority apt for the atmosphere, alliteration gives emphasis to the poem's meaning. The stillness of the ancient house, the movement of the snakes and the frozen air suggest despair and feeling of being abandoned. Thus, the sound devices, while bringing in euphony intensifies what is already there in the semantic plane.

It was said in the previous chapter that a rhetorical question does not demand an answer. Leech says that "it is a positive question which is understood as if equivalent to a negative statement."[26] The rhetorical question which is spread in the last four lines of the poem announces the speaker's feelings. The negation that appears in lines 12-13 ("you cannot believe, darling / can you,") carries weight, because it forecasts the negative reply the listener might give. The rhetorical question underlines the emotional state created by the absence of love. The feeling created in this way is not particular; it engulfs the reader too and is thus universal.

In "Evening at the old Nalappat House" the poet presents a haunted evening : the ghost of memories visiting the speaker bringing with it tender love for man and nature. The poem evokes feelings for the lost world in the reader too. Once again sound pattern is seen to do the job of importing vigour to the poem's meaning.

Evening at the Old Nalapat House

1. No lamps are lit at the Nalapat House
2. When the first star comes, only the fireflies
3. Light up the stone steps and their potted plants.
4. The only servant who caretakes, cycles
5. In the evenings to the warm well-lit
6. Bazar, only my grandmother walks there
7. Then, though dead for eighteen years and wispy
8. As a shred of mist, walks on the white sand
9. Of the courtyard where she watched us play as
10. Children, a long long time ago, walks through
11. The barred doors, all brass-knobbed and dark and

12. Climbs the stairs scaring even the civets,
13. The bats and the insane rats, clambers up to peer
14. Out through loose hinged windows at the roots of
15. Old trees all cut down and sold, thick roots like
16. Truncated necks wrapped in the lichen of
17. A dozen monsoons and sighs. The fieldhands,
18. Returning home with baskets on their heads,
19. Hear that sigh and speed, their thin legs crushing
20. The weeds the shrubs, their ankles bruised by
21. Thorns, their inside bruised by memories...

The opening lines of the poem build the setting for the visit of the ghost to the ghostly old house standing in the stillness of the dark evening. The twinkle of the first star and the fireflies add to the description of the evening. It is in such evenings that the ghost of the speaker's affectionate grandmother visits her earthly abode.

The ghost is wispy like a shred of mist. Assonance and internal rhyme accentuate the weirdness created by its movement. Still, alliteration is the chief mood maker among the phonological devices noticeable in the poem. In the first ten lines alliteration occurs in the following manner ·

Lines
1. No lamps...lit...Nalapat : /l/, /n/
2. Stone steps...potted plants : /s/, /p/
4. servant...cycles : /s/
5. warm...well-lit : /w/
7. then though : /ð/
8. walks...white : /w/
9. Where...watched : /w/
10. long long : /l/

The time difference between the present and the past when the grand mother lived is specified as eighteen years in line seven. Defamliarization is brought by making this time of infinite length by the expression "a long ling time ago". Here verbal repetition, alliteration of /l/ and assonance of /ð/ add to the unusualness created. The unrestrained movement of the ghost and the way she is received by the present inhabitants of the house are beautifully captured in the following lines.

> ....walks through
> The barred doors, all brass-knobbed and dark and
> Climbs the stairs scaring even the civets,
> The bats and the insane rats........

While giving life to the lifeless by making it sigh at the pitiful condition of the house and the surroundings, Kamala Das attempts to make the ghost not a fearsome thing but the invisible spirit of nature which is the symbol of love and preservation. It is when the grandmother's ghost peers out through the "loose hinged windows" at the tree stumps that she sighs. The stumps covered with lichens are likened to the necks of men choped off by killers and wrapped in cloth — a very powerful poetic rendering of the disfiguring of nature through deforestation. The ghost of the grandmother is thus made to grieve at the sight of the ghost of the once beautiful countryside. The peasants returning from the fields hear the sigh and speed up, partly out of fear and partly out of old memories.

The poem can be compared to "No Noon at Village Home" (CPI) where the same atmosphere prevails. The "sleep walking trees / with owls on their shoulders" create the poem's supernatural atmosphere.

The series of images that depict the ghost and the surroundings present, apart from other details, two mental states of the speaker : those days of the past when she loved someone and was loved by someone and the present in which she suffers the loss of that love. Only the ghost of that love visits her in the silent evenings.

The progression from the remembered experience of the speaker to the experience of other people is marked in the last five lines. The peasants returning home have "their insides bruised by memories...." and thus share unwittingly the experience of the speaker.

The gradual emergence of the non-personal was noticed in

the foregoing. In "Anamalai Poems, No. VIII" the point of concern is the awareness of existence and nonexistence : the dominant thought is about that 'superior love' which enables a being to dissolve into the spirit of the universe.

The Anamalai Poems, No. VIII

1. There is a love greater than all you know
2. that awaits you where the red road finally ends
3. Its patience, proverbial; not for it
4. the random caress or the lust that ends in languour.
5. Its embrace is truth and it erases
6. even the soul's ancient indentations so that
7. some unknown womb shall begin to convulse
8. to welcome your restructured perfection.

The poem is in the form of an address to everyone including the poet herself. Death is defined as the greater love which awaits everyone where the symbolic red road finally ends. 'Death' is the ultimate reality, it is unique and it equalizes everyone. Such details of death as subject matter for poetry are out of fashion today. The important aspect of the poem that catches the reader's attention is the remarkable change noticeable in the attitude of the poet. The equation of love with death shows development in the attitude.

The prominent linguistic feature of this poem is that all its verbs are in simple present : "There is a love... you know/that awaits you... the red road finally ends./Its patience (is) proverbial... that ends... its embrace.... it erases.... shall begin to convulse....." The absence of present progressive tense indicates that the poem does not deal with actions developing through time. The first line itself shows that the poet's intention is to say something of the nature of a universal truth : the existence of something that has been revealed to her after years of struggle. It tells the readers, whom she apparently addresses, about the existence of a superior kind of love. Since the object being described is an abstraction, it brings in the notion of the existence and validity of that which has no concrete equivalent. What line 2 of the poem implicates is clear : by equating love with death she has made a strange diversion from the earlier attitude. A prose rendering of the poem, while showing how the deviant pattern of the original text is aesthetic, will help clarify the message :

> A love, so far unknown to the poet, waits for her where the red road ends. Its patience is proverbial. It demands neither fondling nor lust that ends in exhaustion. It embraces only truth and perfection. It erases the ancient marks and figures from the soul. On meeting this love, an unknown womb will whirr with new life. This womb will welcome the self and its restructured perfection.

In the third line of the poem Kamala Das's speaker says that the "patience" of this superior love is "proverbial". This implicates that this "love" is not restrained by time and the statement about its power to erase every scar establishes the fact that she is speaking about a truth which is beyond time. Hence, as S.J. Keyser notes in his analysis of the poems of Wallace Stevens[27] the use of simple present expresses general truth which is timeless. In sum, Kamala Das's speaker is telling about a state which is free from human intervention. To this general truth she adds what is truth for the Hindus and Budhists : the truth of rebirth. She seems to believe that things do not end with the perishing of the body. Her intension seems to be to look beyond the old rotting body or the funeral pyre.[28]

The interplay of the personal and the non-personal was noted in the foregoing discussion; in the succeeding pages the non-personal thoughts of the poet will be highlighted. This will complete the study of the dialectics of individuality and universality seen in the poetry of Kamala Das. The poem "Nani" (*Old Playhouse and Other Poems*) is one that condemns the lack of feeling for fellow beings.

Nani

1. Nani the pregnant maid hanged herself
2. In the privy one day. For three long hours
3. Until the police came, she was hanging there,
4. A clumsy puppet, and when the wind blew
5. Turning her gently on the rope, it seemed

6. To us who were children then, that Nani
7. Was doing to delight us, a comic
8. Dance.... The shrubs grew fast. Before the summer's end,
9. The yellow flowers had hugged the doorway
10. And the walls. The privy, so abandoned,
11. Became an altar then, a lonely shrine
12. For a goddess who was dead. Another
13. Year or two, and, I asked my grandmother
14. One day, don't you remember Nani, the dark
15. Plump one who bathed me near the well? Grandmother
16. Shifted the reading glasses on her nose
17. And stared at me. Nani, she asked, who is she?
18. With that question ended Nani. Each truth
19. Ends thus with a query. It is this designed
20. Deafness that turns mortality into
21. Immortality, the definite into
22. The soft indefinite. They are lucky
23. Who ask questions and move on before
24. The answers come, those wise ones who reside
25. In the blue silent zone, unscratched by doubts
26. For their's is the clotted peace embedded
27. In life, like music in the Koel's egg,
28. Like lust in blood, or like the sap in a tree...

The poem which is a typical example of free verse has no stanzas, but has long drawn out lines. Though the lines are not richly foregrounded, they constitute original metaphorical language. The time of action in the first eighteen lines is set in the past when the speaker was a child. In these eighteen lines are given the story of the poem : the suicide of a maid called Nani. In the remaining lines the poet views the incident from the elevated position of a humanist.

Nani is the symbol of every woman who is the victim of the social system. On the one hand the poem asserts the women's right to live — it is fear of public opinion that compelled Nani to commit suicide. On the other it criticizes the common apathy towards the poor victims of injustice.

It was in a privi that the maid hanged herself. The first eight lines picture the nighmarish sight in a soft vein. The reader receives a sudden jolt when the privy which connotes ugliness is transformed into a shrine, the symbol of sanctity and purity and Nani to its goddess. This attempt at defamiliarization has the effect of a stab at the indifference of everybody. From the author's part this serves as a strong method of expressing resentment at the society's evil ways of seeing things. The deviance seen in these lines makes original metaphors — it is in metaphor that lie the "life-principle of poetry" and "the poet's chief test and glory."[29]

In line 17 the fact Nani existed is negated by one who knew her. This negation calls for further evaluation of human attitude towards fellow beings. Kamala Das views the process of pushing the painful incidents into oblivion as an endless process which is indicative of the lack of feeling for those who suffer. Those who throw things to forgetfulness are called the "free" and the "wise" — euphemisms for the cold and dispassionate view of life.

Social norms induced the deadly shame in Nani. For the poet Nani is the symbol of all the victims of society's cruelty and lack of sympathy. In a wider context the fate of Nani might be the fate of every woman and in a still wider context it is the fate of the weakest among humanity. Horror and amusement, the two opposing states of mind, are created through the foregrounded paradigm denoting death and movements of the dead body : "hanged" "hanging", "turning", "comic dance", "clumsy puppet" and "delight". In a similar vein "privy" a noun that suggests ugliness is juxtaposed to "shrine" that suggests sanctity. The foregrounded nouns "maid", "puppet", "goddess", "privy", "altar", and "shrine" show the interplay of the human and the divine. While the noun "maid" calls attention to the woman who had an individuality of her own, "puppet", shows what has become of her. "Privy" stands for the disgusting reality; "goddess" "alter" and "shrine" suggest meaningless mystification after everything had ended in the most disastrous manner. Time is represented by the following foregrounded items : "One day," "three long hours", "summer", "another year or two" and "one day" The shame and pain that Nani's hanging body represent merge with the cold and dispassionate attitude of man in general as meaning of the foreground elements develop.

The shift from the particular to the universal begins with the construction of unusualness — the transformation of the "privi" into a shrine; but it is actually done with the embeded dialogue, a noticeable turn in the style of the poem. The values of the lexical items "mortality" and "definite", "immortality" and "indefinite" show the strength of the last part of the poem (lines 18-28). Though it seems to be not very easy to explain the syntactic relation of these items, the general sense is clear. Man in general is the victim of the belief that his own life is unique; reality remains submerged in willed forgetfulness. All the time man ignores truths about life and values to be honoured. Thus, people who wilfully ignore things that are not directly related to them remain in the "blue silent zone" of wisdom. However, the last three lines with three comparisons in them stand out : "For theirs is the clotted peace embedded/ In life, like music in Koel's egg, / Like lust in blood, or like the sap in a tree...." Nothing special is added to the meaning of the poem by these similes. Hence it is felt that the poem would have gained without them.

Lack of feeling for the fellow beings is viewed from another angle in "Cochin's Jewish Quarter" (*Indian Literary Review,* 3, 2, 1985- hereafter ILR). The style is different from that of "Nani" because here the poet's purpose is to show the direction of actions and events.

COCHIN'S JEWISH QUARTER

1. Walking the cobbled lane in Cochin's Jewish Quarter,
2. I watched the evening's sun slant against shuttered faces,
3. Pale, gleaming at dark doorways like a bouquet
4. Of some unfragrant bloom, and walked on, uneasy as

5. I always seemed to be in unsmiling towns, hearing
6. An old dog moan, resting its head on the window sill.
7. And glancing in, I saw a man lie there, slowly dying
8. With a twitch of his loosened mouth and a rolling of
9. His eyes; there was no one else in the room but the dog.
10. He was perhaps dying of some fearsome pox alone
11. In a cluttered room with just one window that faced
12. The shadowed east. I wished I had a mirror then to offer
13. Him the face of the sun, the small cold face of an autumn sun
14. Or, at least the courage to sit holding his poor
15. Failing hands. Coward that I was and civilised
16. To suit the age I entered an antique shop
17. With a neat rapid stride and in the rasping voice
18. Of the greedy, bargained for a ming....

The sequence of events in the poem is set in an evening at a lane in Cochin. The specification of the exact place and time gives factual accuracy to the events described. The pale beams of the setting sun (likened to a bouquet made of unfragrant flowers), the unfamiliar town and the uneasiness of the speaker provide the setting for the unpleasant theme of the poem. The "moaning" of the dog, a cry of distress, is for the people of Kerala an omen announcing the impending visit of the messenger of the god of truth and death.

When the poet describes the dying man — the twitch on his mouth, the rolling of his eyes, the cluttered room in which he was lying and his lone companion, the dog — in a transparent language the experience is transferred to the sensitive reader too. The poet's wish to throw the reflection of the "small cold face of the autumn sun" or to soothe him is defeated by inherent cowardice. Identifying this cowardice with the ways of the civilized people the poet once again hints at the deterioration in moral standards among humanity.

The sequence of verbs describes two simultaneous actions : the speaker moving and the man dying. The rhythm of physical movement is close to the rhythm of the gasping of the man. The world at large, it is to be inferred, is busy with their own affairs while a few among them suffer miserably. It is implied in the end of the poem that people pretend to be busy. In this poem the speaker herself is the person who wilfully ignores the poor sufferer. This attitude in a way reminds us of the grandmother's attitude in "Nani". The progression of events are given in the progressive form ('be' deleted) of the verbs :

glancing (the poet)
slowly dying (the man)
rolling (the man's eyes)
dying (the man)
Holding (the poet's wish)
failing (the man's hands)
rasping (the poet's voice)

Thus the verbs in progressive form carry the subject matter of the poem. The progressive aspect of the verbal system accounts for the events taking place within the poem's world as well as in the world of reality. The tense system helps the presentation of the simultaneous action of the poet's movement and the death of the poor man with his grieving animal friend beside him. Here the poet brings home, once again, the fact that human beings wear the mask of magnanimity while in reality they cannot go beyond the limits imposed by their own ego. The image of the brooding dog serves as an attention calling device : it calls attention to the antipathy of those who enjoy comfort, towards the unfortunate.

The progression of the temporal events is seen to assume a different magnitude when we read between the lines. An incident which a layman would forget as time passes has become, under the hands of the poet, an instrument to measure human values. Thus, taking a not very serious event such as the death of a poor man from the every day life Kamala Das projects the lack of compassion among human beings.

The depiction of individual's response to reality was the main motto of the poems discussed above. In the succeeding one ("The Inheritance" (OP) Kamala Das handles the disfiguring function of religion in Indian society.

THE INHERITANCE

1. This then was our only inheritance, this ancient
2. Virus that we nurtured in the soul so
3. That when at sundown, the Muezzin's high wail sounded from
4. The mosque, the chapel-bells announced the angelus, and
5. From the temple rose the Brahmin's assonant chant, we
6. Walked with hearts grown scabrous with a hate, illogical,
7. And chose not to believe — what we perhaps vaguely sensed.
8. That it was only our father's lunacy speaking,
9. In three different tones, babbling : Slay them who do not
10. Believe, or better still, disembowel their young ones
11. And scatter on the streets the meagre innards. Oh God,
12. Blessed be your fair name, blessed be the religion
13. Purified in the unbelievers blood, blessed be
14. Our sacred city, blessed be its incarnadined glory....

The use of the plural pronoun "we" indicates the shift from personal to social : the poem in its fourteen lines exposes the paradoxical history of the land that has given birth to and nurtured the children who wound their mother mortally in the name of religions. The mosque, the church and the temple with their different approaches to God and man have divided the society into distinctive groups and have succeeded in keeping people in perpetual antagonism. So the Muezzin's wail, the church bells and the Brahmin's chant sounded in the evenings are not what announce peaceful life but are battle calls of various military regiments that fight for futile cause. Kamala Das brings to the fore the origin of this 'civic strife' with an effective analogy : it is an inherited lunacy that we hear in the evenings' wailings and chants. She seems to maintain this : religion is a virus that we have inherited from our ancestors. The various calls remind us that we are smitten beings.

The fact that the usual association of places of worship is with purity of thought and deed brings in a contradiction in the beginning of the poem which is maintained throughout. The contradiction develops into bitter irony when in lines 9-11 the poet says that the various calls invoke demonic delight in the believers. "Slay", "disembowel", and "scatter on streets the merge innards" are expressions that suggest the demonic designs of those that claim divinity. Thus, it is implied that high moral values and the institution of religion are in antagonistic relationship. In the last four lines the poet imitates the language of liturgy :

> O God,
> Blessed be your fair name, blessed be the religion
> Purified in the unbeliever's blood, blessed be
> Our sacred city, blessed be its incarnadined glory.

The introduction of the metapersonal language (of liturgy) to condemn religions emphasizes the paradox of the poem. Each segment of this "chant" falls like a blow on the religions of human race.

Kamala Das, in one of her books in Malayalam, says that she is a preacher of the religion called love and that all religions other than "love" are executioners. In this book she argues that India is not secular and should India exist, she should officially ban religions : instead of waging wars India should eliminate the moral poison called religion from her blood-stream.[30]

The poems taken for analysis till this point have been found to emanate a typically graceful energy. However, this is not always the case. Next, we shall examine another poem treating the non-personal theme — "The Flag" (SC) — but which is a failure as a piece of art.

THE FLAG

1. The orange stands for fire, for fire that eats
2. Us all in the end....
3. The white stands for purity we dream and

Never find

The green stands for pastures of paradise
Where even the poor

May have a place. The wheel in the centre
Stationery, stands

For what else but time, arrested falsely
By human hands? Dear
Flag, look, beneath you the scarred limbs of this
City sprawl, scarred so

Emaciated... and yet how grandly
The ornaments gleam !

The neons wink, the harlots walk, swaying
Their wasted hips, the

Rich men dance with one another's wives and
Eke out a shabby,

Secret ecstacy, and, poor old men lie
In wet pavements and
Cough, cough their lungs out. Yet there is whiskey
In the breath of winds.

And Channel Number Five, and the cooking's
Smell. Poor flag, dear one,

Your pride is lost, it is time to leave the sky
And fall, fall and hide

Your shame beneath this blood-drenched Indian soil
And lie there and rot

As those poor babies who die of hunger
And are buried, rot.....

It is time to say good bye to your charms
Dear, to your old,

Meaningless pride, to your crude postures of
Honour, to the lies

Your colours tell to the false hopes you did

36. Extend, to your old
37. Macabre dance in the blueness of our sky...

The poem is about the poor people of India who lead a hard and miserable life. The picture of Independent India presented is naturalistic : the prominence of the syntactic items denoting corruption, poverty, disease and death explain the pitiful state of the poor. The flag, which is the symbol of national pride, in reality symbolizes shame.

The metaphorical expressions and imagery take the reader to streets, pavements and huts where corruption and death are quite commonplace. The following units speak about the poor :

Scarred limbs of the city sprawl
harlots walk swaying their wasted hips
oldmen lie in wet pavements and cough
poor babies die of hunger

The sufferings of the poor people are juxtposed to the luxurious life of the rich. The following units explain this :

Ornaments gleam
neons wink
rich men dance with one another's wives
whiskey in the breath of winds

Standing above the two apparently contradictory states is the symbol of pride and prosperity, the tricolour flag. When the flag does its "macabre dance" the irony becomes all the more clear. The flag is not the symbol of unity and equality, but of descrimination and segmentation. In other words, the three colours of the flag do not symbolize purity, prosperity and truth, they rather stand for the denial of these things. Hence, the flag is not qualified to flutter in the Indian air : it should falls and rot with the rotting babies of the poor Indians.

However, the language of the poem which purports these sentiments is different from those we have analysed. J.P. Thorne has contended that in poetry surface structure variation without variation in deep structure is bad style. It was observed in the previous chapter that poems also have a poetic structure, which often varies in the same poet. The mere variation in surface structure (of the lines) or the mere change in poetic structure does not produce good poetry. Oddness, ofcourse, is a mark of deviance but in "The Flag" the oddness in lines 1, 9, 10, 12 is only superficial. It is not distinctively deviant from the standard language to be poetic. The repetitions "for fire, for fire" in the first line, "cough, cough" in line 21 and "fall, fall" in line 26 are but part of this superficiality. Even the contrast noted in the beginning is not subtle. The theme is quite commonplace and a sincere attempt at defamiliariztion is seen nowhere. Hence critical remarks on the poem such as "The Flag'... gives free rein to the poet's liberal imagination... The scheme of couplets articulates fully the rhythm and movement of the verse...."[31] are banal. Further, it is seen that the use of ellipses does not carry the usual weight — in this poem ellipses seem to degenerate into "three lazy dots".[32]

The theme of this poem however transcends the theme of love and personal sorrows discussed in detail in the previous chapter. The total absence of the personal element is an important aspect of this and a few other of the poems we have taken for study in this chapter. However, the poem being one among Kamala Das's earlier pieces, does not mark any noticeable change in the poet's approach. Instead, it shows that feeling for the sufferers was already there and as time progressed the poet's own view of life changed. An Examination of "Sepia" (SC) will throw more light upon the message of this poem.

SEPIA

1. It's to hold anger
2. Like a living sun
3. And scorch
4. Scorch to the very marrow
5. This sad mouthed human
6. Race.

7. Dehydrate this open hunger
8. Clog the dry, tangled veins
9. With what else,
10. But moss. And, enough enough
11. They have just had enough
12. Of everything.

13. Even dreams are flat
14. And sepia.
15. They fade with chlorophyll
16. Under harsh bathroom lamps,
17. In noon-day queues, they dream
18. Of limbs and limousins;
19. They do not go up the trees
20. To reach with finger tips
21. A frings of summer clouds;
22. They do not go down the sea
23. To count the mermaids eggs
24. That lie beneath the
25. Anemones. No they have not
26. Learnt to believe
27. In things they do not see
28. Or hear.

29. They are faceless, many-cousined,
30. Sad, they rush at every call
31. They only sulk in privacy;
32. Their religion?
33. The newspaper-hate, the bulge
34. In wallets, the scent of morning tea,
35. And ofcourse,
36. Of course, the week-ends
37. Tired lust.

38. Are they the distinguished
39. Human race?
40. Enough, enough, they have just had
41. Enough of everything,
42. Let anger grow like a living sun
43. And scorch,
44. Scorch to the very marrow,
45. This sad mouthed human
46. Race.

Kamala Das begins the poem with a comparison : "anger" is compared to "a living sun". Further she thinks of holding it and using it as an instrument to scorch the humanity "to the very marrow''. There might be several suns in the universe and they might die, still the poet's comparison of anger with ''a living sun'' might have a meaning which is not clear in the first few lines.

In lines 7-8 the poet issues two commands to a supposed audience, or to the reader : ''Dehydrate this open hunger /Clog the dry, tangled veins''. Similar situations have been dealt with in Chapter Three and it was noted that such commands cannot be genuine. Then what is the impact of the imperatives on the reader? The poet is commanding to ''dehydrate this open hunger'' and to ''clog the dry tangled veins.'' Then she expresses her hesitation with what else / But moss'' and thus mitigates the illocutionary force of the command. It is true that the absurd too is meaningful in poetry. Still, how can we account for the absurdities noted above? The next four lines are statements : ''Even dreams are flat / And sepia'' and under the harsh bathroom lamps they fade with chlorophyll. Whose dreams? Can we connect dreams with chlorophyll and photosynthesis? These lines too do not submit themselves for a clear interpretation.

In line 17 the way the third person plural pronoun ''they'' is put to use differs from its earlier occurrence in line 15. In line 15 the pronoun ''they'' has the antecedent ''sepia''. But in line 17 the antecedent of ''they'' might be the ''sad mouthed human race'' of lines 5 and 6. Hence the ''sad mouthed human race'' should be understood as dreaming of ''limbs'' (sex!) and ''limousins'' (cars!). Lines 19-28 contain a series of negatives helping to define this segment of humanity — who might be the rich and the aimless — by the technique of exclusion. Kamala Das tells her readers that these people do not have a progressive outlook. She says that the rich are idle and unimaginative : ''they do not go up the tree'', ''they do not go down the sea,'' ''they have not/Learnt to believe/In things they do not see.'' The reader knows what these suggest. However, the significance of the comparison, commands and assertions is yet not clear.

In lines 29-46 Kamala Das defines the rich Indians in the affirmative suggesting the opposite : they are ''faceless,'' ''many cousined'' and timid, they hate news papers, they have wallets full of money and ofcourse lust is a part their life. In lines 38-39 she puts a question : ''Are they the distinguished/Human race?'' It appears that the poet is in doubt. In the succeeding lines she says that they are a complacent group. The poem ends in refrain — the opening lines are repeated. Still, as far as interpretation is concerned, we are almost where we began. We must, therefore, say that the poem lacks coherence.

Though this poem cannot be listed among the good poems of Kamala Das, it is clear enough that she is condemning the idle rich. The rich like immobility while the rest of the world yearns for a change. Thus, according to the poet the rich are unaware of time and apprehensive of change. The anger of the suffering multitude, like the burning sun, should burn those sepia down and march ahead. Kamala Das, though an aristocrat by birth thus identifies herself with the suffering millions.

The apparent lack of coherence of "Sepia" is compensated for in "Speech" (CPI) which depicts the plight of a section of humanity in an opaque style.

Speech

1. Lyre strings
2. Earth's network of veins
3. And piano keys,
4. Each livened pulse;
5. Wind's finger tips
6. Twang,
7. Percuss the pulse
8. Rain but drums,
9. And trees,
10. Their repose
11. Aquiver,
12. Rot within,
13. The lichen
14. Their only speech.

Taken out of the context the poem as a whole may be visualised as a complex image evoking the scene of a mimical show : the rain is drumming, the whole earth is vibrant, everything is music and speech is reduced to nothing (in the expression "The lichen/Their only speech.") In this way inarticulation itself becomes articulation in this poem. But intertextuality validates the observation that the poem is about the people who are ignored and oppressed by the fortunate and the affluent.

"Lyre strings", "piano keys" and "drums" suggest music and dance. "Rain", "trees", and "lichen" have their associations with nature. "Finger tips", "pulse", "repose" and "speech" must have their legitimate associations with human beings who must be the focus to which the nonhuman aspects converge. The connection of inanimate forces like wind and rain with music is reminiscent of T.S. Eliot's technique of "sudden contrast of associations which produces a powerful effect". But how does meaning arise out of such connections? For an answer we have to look into certain of the poem's phonological aspects also.

The prominence of the voiceless /s/ "possesses a range of potential suggestability"[33] when supported by meaning. This suggests other classes of sounds such as in "hissing", "sighing" and "whispering". It is intuitively understood that the speech thematised here is almost incoherent — it is indistinguishable from the sound of falling rain drops and the hissing of the wind. Hence, the prominence of /s/ suggests that the focus of the poem is the "voicelessness" of the oppressed group.

The interlacing of the several kinds of phonological repetition — liquid consonant /l/, nasal /n/ and voiced /z/ and voiceless /s/ — gives the poem the pattern that enriches its meaning. "Twang" representing the sound of a string being pulled and released is onomatopoeic. The speech of the people who are not physically represented in the poem is like sighs or mere whisper. The /s/ and /z/ sounds with which lines 1-5 and 7-10 (effecting pararhyme) illustrate this. The lines run on :

Strings
veins

keys
pulse
tips
......
pulse
drums
trees
repose

The connection of the reader with the 'speakers' is made not only through the ear but also through the empathical experience of the physical sensations carried by expressions such as "Earth's network of veins" and "livened pulse" and through the concurrent appeal to more than one sense such as "lyre strings" and "piano keys" which carry the sensation of the sight of their trunk and the green colour. The following words of Yeats will make our observations further clear :

> All sounds, all colours, all forms, either because of their pre-ordained energies of because of long association, evoke indefinable and yet precise emotions, or as I prefer to think, call down among us certain disembodied powers, whose foot steps over our hearts we call emotions; and when sound, and colour, and form are in musical relation to one another, they become as it were one sound, one colour one form, and evoke and emotion that is made out of their distinct evocations and yet is one emotion.[34]

Thus the emotion evoked in this poem has direct relations with the human beings ignored by the fortunate segment of humanity. The underlying idea in "Speech", therefore, is in consonance with the generality of the themes brought to light in this chapter. The same attitude prevails in "The House Builders" (CPI) also.

The House Builders

1. The cicadas in brambled foliage
2. Naturally concave. So also these

3. Men who crawl up the cogged scaffoldings
4. Building houses for the alien rich.
5. Some days the hot sky flings at us scraps
6. Of Telugu songs and we intently
7. Listen, but we wait in vain for the harsh
8. Message of the lowly. In merry tunes
9. Their voices break, but just a little, as
10. Though the hero's happiness is too big
11. A burden on their breath, too big a lie
12. For their throats to swallow, but past sunset
13. Their jest sounds ribald, their lusts seem robust
14. Puny, these toymen of dust, fathers of light
15. Dust children but their hands like the withered boughs
16. Of some mythic hoodoo tree cast only
17. Cool shadows and with native grace bestow
18. Even on unbelievers, vast shelters.

The poem begins with a very good comparison through parallel placement of ideas : the cicadas clouching the "brambled foliage" are concave naturally, and the house builders who clutch the bamboo scaffoldings too are concave, not naturally but due to hard work. The soft musical tone of the lines indicates that it is in a soft vein that she describes the life style of the poor workers who construct buildings for the "alien rich". Any one who happens to see such workers at work will know that this song has a touch of reality.

Almost all sound devices that make a verse composition musical seem to be employed in this poem. Stephen Ullmann has noted the association of the liquid consonant /l/ with the impression of softness citing examples from different languages[35]. Alliteration of plosives /k/ and /b/, internal rhyme and pararhyme with plosive /t/ suggest, impressionistically, a hard note on the scale. Connection can be established with the soft musical tone with which the poet 'sings' and the coarseness of the ribald of the workers on the abstract level of sound symbolism. The sonorous vowel /eu/ in line seventeen also is indicative of the quality of the voice of the workers.

The prominence of /l/ phoneme effects phonological foregrounding which explains the mood of the poet — lightness of the sounds suggests the light heartedness with which the poet signs about the workers. The /l/ phoneme occur in the following way :

Lines :

1. brambled foliage
2. naturally.... also
3. crawl... scaffoldings
4. building... alien
5. flings
6. Telugu... intently
7. listen
8. lowly
9. little
10. lie
11. swallow
12. ribald...lusts
13. light
14. children...like
15. only
16. cool
17. unbelievers...shelters.

The poem is about the workers who toil from dawn to dusk to earn a living. The poor people who work hard for the "alien rich"— the rich of their own nation who are psychospatially remote and so alien to them — are viewed as capable of casting "cool shadows...even on unbelievers".

The image of the cicadas suggests that the workers are paltry creatures of the earth; they laugh and live a life of their own, unperturbed by what happens in the world of the "alien rich". The songs they sing while at work are either about the lives of rich men or about the exploits of a hero. The following lines offer a fine contrast to what the workers themselves stand for :

> ....In merry tunes
> Their voices break, but just a little, as
> Though the hero's happiness is too big
> A burden on their breath,...

After the day's work, after sunset, they find solace in "ribald" and "robust lust". The plight of the downtrodden is further emphasized by calling them the "toymen of dust" for whom earthly life is but an endless stretch of hard work, ribald and procreative acts. However their ill-looking hands are useful to the rest of humanity, because those hands, like the branches of a mythical hoodoo tree, cast cool shadows even on those who have no faith in their usefulness. The way the meaning of this poem is understood might help comprehend the thoughts contained in "The Return of Hitler" (ILR, 3, 2, 1985).

The Return of Hitler

1. After July, in Colombo there were
2. No Tamils in sight, no arangetrams
3. Were held in the halls, no flower-seller
4. Came again to the door with long strings
5. Of jasmine to perfume the ladies' hair.
6. Like rodents they were all holed up in fear,
7. Their smell began to resemble the rats',
8. A mixture of dung, copper and potash,
9. They were the hunted, they cowered behind
10. Doors, in the murky twilight of their rooms,
11. The whites of their eyes, glimmering like pearls.
12. Hitler rose from the dead; he demanded
13. Yet another round of applause; he hailed
14. The robust Aryan blood, the sinister
15. Brew that absolves a man of his sins and
16. Gives him the right to kill his former friends.

17. The dark Dravidian laid his three year old child
18. On his lap, little mother, he said, close your eyes and sleep....

This poem is a slightly changed version of "After July" which appears in Kamala Das's *Collected Poems Vol. 1.* The title, two words ("long" in line four and "cried" in the last line) and two punctuation marks constitute the change. The subject matter of the poem is the ethnic problem in Sri Lanka.

Time and place, the canvas on which the poet portrays the malignance of those who subject others to cruelty in the name of race and colour are given in the first line itself : "After July in Colombo...." This means that the temporal event that forms the subject matter of the poem occurs in Sri Lanka. The first line unfolds the gamut of events that trigged the disastrous civil war in Sri Lanka. Thus the reference to the time and place works as a foregrounding device which unfolds before the reader the oppression and the resultant rage which ended in 'civic strife'.

In the first five lines the disruption of peace and the fear of the Sri Lankan Tamils are shown by the suggestion of disruption in their routine activities. The terms indicating the harmonious life of the Tamils are "arangetrams" which means maiden dance performance and "strings of Jasmine" which is almost a part of the Tamil women's hair. "Arangetrams" and jasmine flowers are associated with the aesthetics of the Tamil Community. Thus the tow negations in line 2 and 3 indicate the breaking up of harmony; in the remaining lines the poet replaces it (harmony) with horror.

The comparison of the Tamils with rodents explains the inhuman atrocities to which they were subjected to by the Sinhalese who claim an Aryan descent. The comparison of the Tamils' body odour with that of rats intensifies the horror of the situation. The jasmine flowers which emit fragrance is contrasted with "dung, copper and potash" that contaminate the air. The Tamils are "holed up" like rodents and they cower as if chased by snakes.

The function of "overtones associated with name" was noted in the discussion of Kamala Das's treatment of Krishna myth. In "The Return of Hitler" the overtone associated with the name

Hitler suggests not a myth but a stark reality. The clinical brutality of Hitler and his Nazi followers is still alive in the memory of the world. Thus Kamala Das pictures the horror of the Sri Lankan Tamils in the following way : "Hitler rose from the dead; he demanded/Yet another round of applause; he hailed/The robust Aryan blood..."

The whole picture of the horror of the Tamils is given in parallel clauses describing Hitler's resurrection and his demand for another stretch of cruelty. Hitler rising from the grave to command Aryan supremacy once again and the trembling black dravidian present the two images that suggest the primordial fear of evil forces of nature ruling the earth upon the abolition of the creative mind of man. The phrase "robust Aryan blood" stylistically and thematically relate the poem to "A Certain Defect in the Blood," which is discussed in the coming pages. The lexical item "robust" which appears in "The House Builders" in connection with lust connotes an entirely different meaning here. Here "the robust Aryan blood" is the "sinister /Brew that absolves the man of his sins" — hence the poet seems to say that the sins of the oppressors are robust. The last two lines contain a highly suggestive image : this highlights the helplessness of the Sri Lankan Tamils and the horrid state of affairs which may be disastrous to future generations. A heightened emotion is added to this theme in "A Certain Defect in the Blood" (CPI).

A Certain Defect In the Blood

Fear had wrapped our movements. Like spiders exposed
To a water jet we curled ourselves into
Tight balls, preparing to escape, to escape,
Into sleep and its wide freedom of the soul.
When awake our silence was greater still.
Only the children, undeterred, asked questions
On and on and on, receiving except for
Hard looks, no replies. It was a defect
In our blood that made us the land's inferiors,
A ccrtain muddiness in the usual red,

11. Revealing our non Aryan descent. Then
12. Suddenly, at the whirring of the planes
13. The elders among us pricked up their ears,
14. their hopes reviving for a moment or two.
15. Perhaps in a kinder couontry their stigma
16. Might stay unrecognized and the children might
17. Play again under the benign skies of
18. Summer months, the memories of July '83
19. Growing fainter and fainter as the smoke that
20. Stains the firmament in the wake of a gunshot must.

The poem carries the voice of the oppressed Tamils of Sri Lanka : the impression of the sufferers addressing the poet and the poet rendering the text of their talk in verse is effected using second person narration. Hence the poet's thoughts are undistinguishable from the thoughts of the individuated multitude.

The poem has a stretch of images, all related to the pitiful state in which the Tamils are. The image of the spiders curling when exposed to a water jet suggests the horror the oppressed group experiences. Abstract imagery is noticed in the people's preparation to escape into sleep and wider freedoms of soul. "Muddiness in the usual red" is another figurative expression condemning the racial prejudice of the Sinhala race. The whirring of the planes suggests whirring of hope; we know from reports that the Tamils foolishly believed that the Russians might save them.

Kamala Das presents facts quoting month and year — July ' 83 — and the last three lines give the impression that she is recollecting an incident which she had experienced some time ago. The fading memory and the fading smoke after gunshot effect an apt simile — it gives vent to the interpretation that the poet is protesting against state supported antagonism. The last two lines show that the events and emotions created in the preceding lines are but reflections of the speaker.

The poem's imagery creates an intense emotional situation : the first line introduces the fear that has engulfed the Tamils of

Sri Lanka; the lines that follow picture the present and future of these people.

The key image of the poem is present in the following lines :

> It was a defect
> In our blood that made us the land's inferiors,
> A certain muddiness in the usual red,
> Revealing our non Aryan descent.....

Line 10 is lexically unusual. The poet through defamiliarizing the familiar aspects of human blood refers to the unusualness of the context. The characteristics of human blood are universal. But the blood of the oppressed is to the oppressor muddy, dissimilar and therefore defective.

The agony of the group becomes further evident in their elders' expression of hope when planes whirr in the sky. For a while they fancy that the Russians are there to save them. Irony is implied in this hope because powerful nations always wage wars under the pretext of establishing peace and equality. The image of the spider curling under a jet of water is highly suggestive. It explains the pitiful condition of the group as well as the brutality of their oppressors. It can, therefore, be said that the force of the poem lies in its apt use of metaphorical expression. The creation of forceful metaphorical language is of paramount importance in poetry, because the metaphor is always and for ever its glory and strength. We have witnessed Kamala Das's winning of the 'test' in all except a few of the poems analysed so far.

If there was the desire to merge with the world of flux and events noticeable in the poems analysed in the previous chapter the opposite was witnessed in the preceding discussion. The last poem taken for analysis completes the process, for it expresses the poet's advice and wish to transcend the limits of the body.

Advice to Fellow-swimmers

1. When you learn to swim
2. do not enter a river that has no ocean
3. to flow into, one ignorant of destinations
4. And knowing only the flowing as its destiny,
5. like the weary rivers of the blood

6. that bear the scum of ancient memories,
7. but go swim in the sea,
8. go swim in the great blue sea
9. where the first tide you meet is your body,
10. that familiar pest,
11. but if you learn to cross it
12. you are safe, yes, beyond it you are safe,
13. For, even sinking would make no difference then....

From the point of view of stylistics the importance of this poem rests mainly in the way linguistic resources are exploited. It is evident that Kamala Das is an adept in taking maximum advantage of her repertoire of English vocabulary. A comparison of Kamala Das's poetry with Sylvia Plath's or T.S. Eliot's, though it will not be altogether out of place, will be an attempt that will not yield much desirable result. Both Kamala Das and Plath have distinctively different features that do not allow a worthwhile comparison. It requires the talent and tradition of a poet like Sylvia Plath to create a piece like "Lady Lazarous". Similarly only a poet brought up in a Hindu family can write a poem like "Ghanashyam." However, accidental similarities in themes do exist in the writings of writers belonging to different time and milieu. So the seeming similarity that "Advice to Fellow-swimmers" has with T.S. Eliot's "They Dry Salvages" has to be viewed in this way.

The opening of "The Dry Salvages"[36] creates a feeling similar to the one created in the opening lines of this poem. The rhythmic flow of the river is likened to the flow of Man's life. Man, as his general tendency shows, does not attempt to look beyond the rhythm of his machines. But once he looks beyond it he will be able to understand how the flow of the river from source to mouth is like his journey from past to future. The river ultimately merges with the sea — in most cases — losing its identity, its past and present. So does man as he marches along with time to future, the end of everything is void, a state without direction, time and space.

If what is said above is true of "The Dry Salvages" Kamala

Das's swimmer and river have a little more function : she thinks not only about physical life but also beyond. The poem begins with the temporal clause "when you begin to swim," suggesting at least superficially, the relation of the message to the temporal aspects. However, the progression is from the time consciousness of the corporeal to the timelessness of the ethereal. The syntax enacts this progression. The first temporal clause which contains the main message — the swimming which is symbolic is the progression from mundaneness to formlessness — is extended by the relative clause using "that" in the second line. This is joined to another clause with the pure coordinator "and" in the fourth line. This is followed again by a relative clause in the sixth line and by "but" in the last. Thus, the flow of the river which is a superficial aspect and the process of progression are enacted by the syntax of the poem.

The speech acts performed by the speaker are forbidding (second line) and asserting using comparisons (lines 3-6). Through repetitions of imperatives in the seventh and eighth lines the poet invokes the (absent) listeners to engage in action. Then she tells about the important thing to be done — crossing the tide (which is the metaphor for the body). Once it is crossed the swimmer is safe and "even sinking would make no difference". "Sinking" suggests the disappearance of the plurality implied in the poet's capacity to advise, because if one sinks her individuality disappears. Thus, crossing means over-coming mundaneness and merging with the beatitude of timelessness and formlessness.

"Advice to Fellow-Swimmers" is the last of the poems we have selected for analysis. As the title indicates, the poem is an advice to humanity. In a way it sums up Kamala Das's view of human life. After having experienced pleasure and pain by herself and after watching carefully the way of the world the poet makes deliberations on what appears to be the best approach to life. The poem is thus the symbolic presentation of the abstraction, life, which is unrestrained by the shackles of space and time. Crossing the limitations of body is transcending time and space.

In fine, this Chapter began with the argument that Kamala Das cannot be viewed as an exclusively confessional poet. It was also observed that with her self revealing work she argues for a free life-style for women. This implies that Kamala Das's preoccupation with self forms only one part of her artistry. The analyses conducted in this chapter have shown that her narcissist preoccupations have nothing to do with her love for the fellow women and that upon this emotion is superimposed her love for humanity. In the end even the fading of individuality could be noticed. A close examination of the use of imagery, repetition, parallelism, rhetorical and pragmatic devices, sound devices like alliteration, assonance, consonance and 'motif' and lexical and syntactic elements has given a clear picture of Kamala Das's art and thought. Thus, it is shown that Kamala Das is an artist who is capable of transforming the impulses of the times into poetry. In this way her poetry shows the dialectical presence of individuality and universality.

Notes

1. See Mukařovský, *The Word 154.*
2. Mukařovský, *The Word 155.*
3. Jean Starobinski, "The Style of Autobiography", Chatman 287.
4. Starobinski 290.
5. Views of Donald Davie quoted by Laurence Lerner, "What is Confessional Poetry", *Critical Quarterly* 29, 2 (1987) : 54.
6. Lerner 52.
7. Susan Bassnet, "Textuality/Sexuality", *Essays in Poetics 9.1 (1984) : 4.*
8. See Ullmann, *Meaning* 71.
9. Geoffrey N. Leech, *A Linguistic Guide to English Poetry* (New York : Longman, 1969) 79.
10. Leech, *A Linguistic Guide* 79.
11. Leech, *A Linguistic Guide* 44.
12. Polysyndeton means repetition of conjunctions.
13. A female child offered by her parents to the deity of a temple — thus forsaken — on maturity becomes a dancer at temple performances as well as a concubine. She is thus forced to lead a sad life. The custom still prevails in Karnataka, but has been banned in Kerala, the home state of Kamala Das.
14. See Heidegger 164.
15. See Heidegger 158.
16. Heidegger 311.
17. Heidegger 358.
18. See Leech, *A Linguistic Guide* 93.
19. See Noam Chomsky, *Aspects of Theory of Syntax* (Cambridge, Mass : M.I.T. Press, 1965) 95.

20. Claudio Guillen, "On the Use of Monistic Theories : Parallelism in Poetry," *New Literary History* 18, 3 (1987) : 504.
21. Guillen 505-507.
22. C.f. Leech, *A Linguistic Guide* 99
23. Heidegger 233.
24. Leech, *A Linguistic Guide* 189-91.
25. C.f. Roman Jakobson's views discussed in the second chapter.
26. Leech, A Linguistic Guide 184.
27. See Keyser 100-122.
28. C.f. Kamala Das, *Nisavastram* 44.
29. C.Day Lewis, *The Poetic Image* (1947 ; London : Jonathan Cape, 1969) 17.
30. See Kamala Das, *Nisavastram* 15-18, and 38-39.
31. Rahman 79-80.
32. Hess 40.
33. Leech, A Linguistic Guide 96-97.
34. W.B. Yeats, "Ideas of Good and Evil," *Essays* (London : Macmillan, 1924) 192-93.
35. Stephen Ullmann, *Language and style* (Oxford UP, 1964) 70-71.
36. T.S. Eliot, "The Dry Salvages," *The Complete Poems and plays of T.S. Eliot* (1941; London : Faber and Faber, 1969) 185.

References

Achwal, Madhao B. "The Literary Aspect of Obscenity". *The Roots of Obscenity*. Ed. A.B. Shah. Bombay : Lalvani Publishing House, 1968.

Alphonso Karkala, John B. " 'Gita Govinda' and 'Song of Solomon' ". *Indian Literature* 28.3 (1985) : 95-102.

Anderson, Linda. "At the Threshold of the Self : Woman and Autobiography". *Women's Writings : A Challenging Theory*. Ed. Moira Monteith. Sussex : The Harvester Press, 1986. 54-71.

Austin J.L. *How to do Things with Words*. New York : Oxford UP, 1962.

Bassnet, Susan. "Textuality/Sexuality". *Essays in Poetics* 9.1 (1984) : 1-15.

Bennet, William A. "Linguistics and the Evaluation of Poetic Style". *Journal of Literary Semantics* 10.2 (191) : 95-103.

Bhabha, Homi. "Indo-Anglian Attitudes". *TLS* 21 Apr. 1978 : 445.

Bhattacharji, Sukumari. "A Survey of Sataka Poetry". *Indian Literature* 23.5 (1980) : 12-40.

Blackwell, Fritz. "Krishna Motifs in the Poetry of Sarojini Naidu and Kamala Das." *Journal of South Asian Literature* 13.1-4 (1977) : 9-14.

Bose, Amalendu. "Modern Indian Poetry in English". *Indian Literature* 13.1 (1970) : 51-59.

Chatman, Seymour, ed. *Literary Style : A Symposium*. London : Oxford UP, 1971.

Ching, Marwin K.L., Michael C. Haley, and Ronald F. Lunsford, eds. *Linguistic Perspectives on Literature.* London : Routledge and Kegan Paul, 1980.

Chomsky, Noam. *Aspects of Theory of Syntax*. Cambdirge, Mass : M.I.T. Press, 1965.

Cluysenaar, Anne. *Introduction to Literary Stylistics*. London : Batsford, 1976.

Croce, Bennedetto. *Estetica como scienza dell' espressione e linguistica generale.* Palermo : Sandron, 1913.

Cuddon, J.A. A *Dictionary of Literary Terms*. Delhi : Clarion Books, 1980.

Culler, Jonathan. *Structuralist Poetics : Structuralism, Linguistics and the Study of Literature.* London : Routledge, 1975.

Cureton, Richard D. "E. E. Cummings : A Case Study of Iconic Syntax". *Language and Style.* 14.3 (1981) : 183-215.

Das, Kamala. *Summer in Calcutta*. New Delhi : Everest press, 1965.

—— *The Descendants*. Calcutta : Writers Workshop, 1967.

—— *The Old Playhouse and other Poems*. Madras : Orient Longman, 1973.

—— *Collected Poems* Vol. 1. Trivandrum : The Navakerala Printers, 1984.

—— Interview. *Katha* 86 (1984) : 12-13.

—— "The Anamalai Poems". *Indian Literature* 23.2 (1985) : 45-49.

—— Poetry. *The Indian Literary Review* 3.2 (1985) : 29-33.

—— *Bhayam ente nisavastram*. Calicut : Mathrubumi Printing and Publishing House, 1986.

Datta, Jyotirmoy. "On Caged Chaffinches and Polyglot Parrots". *Quest* Jan.- Mar. 1961; 28-29.

Deshpande, Gauri. *Between Births*. Calcutta : Writers Workshop, 1968.

—— *Lost Love*. Calcutta : Writer's Workshop, 1970.

Dorsch, T.S. *Classical Literary Criticism*. Harmondsworth : Penguin, 1965.

Eliot, T.S. *The Complete Poems and Plays of T.S. Eliot*. 1941. London : Faber and Faber, 1969.

Empson, William. *Seven Types of Ambiguity*. London : Chatto and Windus, 1930.

Enkvist, Nils Erik. *Linguistic Stylistics*. The Hague, Paris : Mouton, 1973.

Epstein, Edmund L. "Non-restrictive Modifiers : Poetic Features of Language". *Studies in English Linguistics*. Ed. Sydney Greenbaum. London : Longman, 1979. 221-34.

Ezekiel, Nissim. *A Time to Change*. London : Fortune Press, 1952.

—— *The Third. Bombay* : The Strand Bookshop, 1959.

—— *The Exact Name*. Calcutta : Writer's Worshop, 1965.

—— *Hymns in Darkness*. Delhi : Oxford UP, 1976.

Fish, Stanley E. "What is stylistics and why are they saying such terrible things about it". *Essays in Modern Stylistics*. Ed. Donald C. Freeman., London : Methuen, 1981.

Foucault, Michel. *The History of Sexuality Vol. 1 : An Introduction*. Trans. Robert Hurley. New York : Random House, 1978.

Frazer, James G. *The Golden Bough : A Study in Magic and Religion*. 1922. New York : Macmillan, 1943.

Freeman, Donald C., ed. *Linguistics and Literary Style*. New York : Holt, Rinehart and Winston, 1970.

Freud, Sigmond. *Collected Papers*, IV. London : Hogarth, 1925.

Gravin, P. *A Prague School Reader on Esthetics, Literary Structure and Style*. Washington : Georgetown UP, 1964.

Grice, H.P. "Logic and Conversation". *Syntax and Semantics, Vol.3 Speech Acts*. Eds. Cole and Morgan. New York : Academic Press, 1975. 41-58.

Guillen, Claudio. "On the use of Monistic Theories : Parallelism in Poetry". *New Literary History* 18.3 (1987) : 497-515.

Haley, Michael C. "Concrete Abstraction : The Linguistic Universe of Metaphor". Ching, Haley and Lunsford 139-54.

Halliday, M.A.K. "Linguistic Function and Literary Style". Chatman, *Literary Style* 330-65.

—— "Descriptive Linguistics and Literary Studies". Freeman 57-72.

Hans, James S. "Presence and Absence in Modern Poetry". *Criticism* 22.4 (1980) : 331.

Heidegger, Martin. *Being and Time*. Trans. John Macquarrie and Edward Robinson. New York : Harper and Row, 1962.

Hess, Linda. "Post-Independence Indian Poetry in English". *Considerations*. Ed. Meenakshi Mukherjee. Bombay : Allied Publishers, 1977. 23-42.

Hough, Graham. *Style and Stylistics*. London : Routledge, 1969.

Iyengar, Srinivasa K.R. *Indian Writing in English*. New Delhi : Sterling, 1984.

Jakobson, Roman. "Closing Statement" : Linguistics and Poetics". *Style in Language*. Ed. T.A. Sebeok. Cambridge, Mass : M.I.T. Press, 1960. 350-77.

Kachru, Braj B, and F. W. Stahlke eds., *Current Trends in Stylistics*. Edmonton : Linguistic Reserch Inc., 1972.

Kalinikova, Elena J. *Indian English Literature : A Perspective*. Ghasiabad : Vimal Prakasan, 1974.

Keyser, Samuel Jay. "Wallace Stevens. Form and Meaning in Four Poems". Freeman 100-122.

King, Bruce. *Modern Indian Poetry in English*. Delhi : Oxford Up, 1987.

Kohli, Devendra, "Passionate Sincerity in Indian Poetry in English". *The journal of Commonwealth Literature* 13.1 (1974) : 23-25.

Krishnamoorthy K, trans. *Vakrokti jeevita of Kuntaka*. Dharwad : Karnataka University, 1977.

Kuykendall, Eleanor, "Breaking the Double Binds". *Language and Style*. 13.4 (1980) : 81-93.

Lakoff., Robin. *Language and Women's place*. New York : Harper Colpohon, 1975.

Leech, Geoffrey N. *A Linguistic Guide to English Poetry*. New York : Longman, 1969.

—— " 'This Bread I Break' — Language and Interpretation". Freeman 119-128.

Leech, Geoffrey N., and Michael M. Short. *Style in Fiction : A Linguistic Introduction to English Fictional Prose*. London : Longman, 1981.

Lemon, L.T., and M. Reis. *Russian Formalist Criticism : Four Essays*, Lincoln : Nebraska UP, 1965.

Lerner, Laurence. "What is Confessional Poetry". *Critical Quarterly* 29.2 (1987) : 46-66.

Levin, Samual R. "Deviation — Statistical and Determinate in Poetic Language". *Lingua* : 12 (1963) : 276-90.

—— "Internal and External Deviation in Poetry". *Word* 21(1965) : 225-237.

Lewis, C. Day *The Poetic Image*. 1947. London : Jonathan Cape, 1969.

Lodge, David, *Language of Fiction*. London : Routledge and Kegan Paul, 1967.

Lunsford, Ronald F. "Byron's Spatial Metaphor : A Psycholinguistic Approach". Ching, Haley and Lunstord 155-59.

Milstead, John. " 'Concrete' and 'Abstract' as Stylistic Descriptors". *Language and Style*. 16.3 (1983) : 284-95.

Mukařovský Jan. "Standard Language and Poetic Language". *Essays on the Language of Literature*. Eds. Seymour Chatman and S.R. Levin. New York : Houghton Mifflin Company, 1967. 241-49.

—— *The Word and the Verbal Art*. Trans. John Burbank and Peter Steiner. New Haven and London : Yale UP, 1977.

Murry, J.M. *Countries of the Mind*. Freeport, N.Y. : Books for Libraries Press, 1968.

Ohmann, Richard. "Generative Grammars and the Concept of Literary Style". *Linguistics and Literary Style*. Ed. Donald C. Freeman. New York : Holt, Rinehart and Winston, 1970. 258-78.

Parthasarathy, R. *Ten Twentieth Century Indian Poets*. Delhi : Oxford UP, 1976.

Peer, W. Van. *Stylistics and Psychology : Investigations of Foregrounding*. London : Croom Helm, 1986.

Rahman, Anisur. *Expressive From in the Poetry of Kamala Das*. New Delhi : Abhinav Publications, 1981.

Ram, Atma. *Interviews with Indian English Writers*. Calcutta : Writer's Workshop, 1983.

Rank, Otto. *Beyond Psychology*. 1941. New York : Dover, 1958.

Riffaterre, Michael. *Semiotics of Poetry*. 1978. London : Methuen, 1980.

Saha. Subhas Chandra. *Modern Indo-Anglian Love Poetry*. Calcutta : Writer's Workshop, 1971.

Saussure, Ferdinand de. *Cours de linguistique générale*. Eds. Charles Bally and Albert Sechehaye. Paris : Payot, 1955.

Searle, J.R. *Speech Acts : An Essay in the Philosophy of Language*. Cambridge : Oxford UP, 1969.

Sidhanta, N.K. "English". *The Indian Literature of Today : A Symposium*. Ed. B. Kumarappa. Bombay : International Book House, 1947. 24-28.

Sinha, Krishna Nandan, Ed. *Indian Writing in English*. New Delhi : Heritage Publishers, 1971.

Sivaramakrishna, M. "The 'Tongue in English Chains' : Indo-English Poetry Today". *Indian Poetry In English : A Critical As sessment*. Eds. Vasant A. Sahane and M. Sivaramakrishna. Madras : Macmillan, 1980. 1-27.

Smith, Barbara Herrnstein. *Poetic Closure : A Study of How Poems End*. Chicago : University of Chicago Press, 1968.

Souza, Eunice de. "Kamala Das, Gauri Deshpande, Mamta Kalia" *Quest* Jan-Feb 1972 : 86-87.

Soyinka, Wole. *Wole Soyinka : Collected Plays* 2. Oxford : OUP, 1974.

Spector, Jack J. *The Aesthetics of Freud : A Study in Psychoanalysis and Art*. London : The Penguin Press, 1972.

Spitzer, Leo. *Linguistics and Literary History : Essays in Stylistics*. Princeton : Princeton UP, 1948.

Srinath. C.N. "Contemporary Indian Poetry in English". *Literary Criterion* 2.3 (1968) : 61-62.

Starobinski, Jean. "The Style of Autobiography". Chatman. *Literary Style* 285-94.

Taylor, Tobolt J. *Linguistic Theory and Structural Stylistics*. Oxford : Pergamon Press, 1980.

Trotter, W.F., trans. *Pense*, By Pascal. New York : Modern Library, 1941.

Ullmann, Stephen. *Language and Style*. Oxford : Oxford UP, 1964.

—— *Meaning and Style*. Oxford : Basil Blackwell, 1973.

Varma, Monika. *Facing Four*. Calcutta : Writer's Workshop, 1973.

Vendler, Helen. Rev. of *Essays on Style and Language*, by Roger Fowler. *Essays in Criticisms* 16 (1966) : 457.

Vossler, Karl. *Frankreichs Kultur in Spiegel seiner Sprachentwick lung.* Heidelberg : Carl Winter, 1913.

Warren, James Perrin. "The Free Growth of Metrical Laws' : Syntactic Parallelism in 'Song of Myself." *Style* 18.1 (1984) : 27-42.

Williams, H.M. *Indo-Anglian Literature, 1800-1970 : A Survey.* Madras : Orient Longman, 1976.

Yeats, W.B. *Essays.* London : Macmillan, 1924.

—— *The Letters of W.B. Yeats.* Ed. Allan Wade. New York : Macmillan, 1955.

Zide, Arlene R.K. Rev. of *The Old Playhouse and Other Poems,* by Kamala Das. *Journal of South Asian Literature* 16.1 (1981) : 233-41.

General Index

T

U

V

W